"As one of the preeminent biblica
qualified to write on the critical
short volume is a clear, concise, bib......., g.........., ... p.........,
the biblical covenants, ideal as a resource for both the church and the academy."
> **Mark L. Strauss,** professor of New Testament, Bethel Seminary

"Simply brilliant! Thomas Schreiner manages to capture both the fine detail and the broad sweep of the covenantal shape of the Bible concisely, faithfully, and irenically. This book may be short, but it is fresh and deeply profound. I know of no better introduction to this vital area of biblical theology. There are, of course, specific areas where readers may disagree with his conclusions, but that doesn't detract from the unique usefulness of this book."
> **Gary Millar,** principal, Queensland Theological College; author, *Calling on the Name of the Lord* and *Saving Eutychus*

"There is nothing like an understanding of the covenants that God makes with his people to open one's eyes to the way God deals with his image bearers. It at once unlocks the whole Bible and makes plain God's way of salvation. Thomas Schreiner brings his theological and biblical acumen to bear upon this topic with the precision of an expert. The result is a fresh and stimulating study of this all-important subject. If you want to grow in faith as you face the future in God's world, then put on your thinking cap and read this book!"
> **Conrad Mbewe**, pastor, Kabwata Baptist Church; chancellor, African Christian University, Lusaka, Zambia

"For twenty-first-century evangelicals, Thomas Schreiner is one of the most trusted names in the field of biblical studies. *Covenant and God's Purpose for the World* is yet another stellar contribution to the church by Schreiner, and it will benefit all who are seeking to better understand the covenants of Scripture."
> **Jason K. Allen**, president, Midwestern Baptist Theological Seminary & College

"Schreiner makes his case with evidence and not theatrics. Ideas are not smuggled in and imposed on texts; rather, Schreiner brings out what a reader can see from Scripture. Is there more to say than this book contains? Of course. And not all readers will affirm all of Schreiner's claims, but given Schreiner's view of old and new covenants in which discontinuity triumphs over continuity, it is hard to imagine a more methodical and succinct presentation."
> **Robert W. Yarbrough,** professor of New Testament, Covenant Theological Seminary

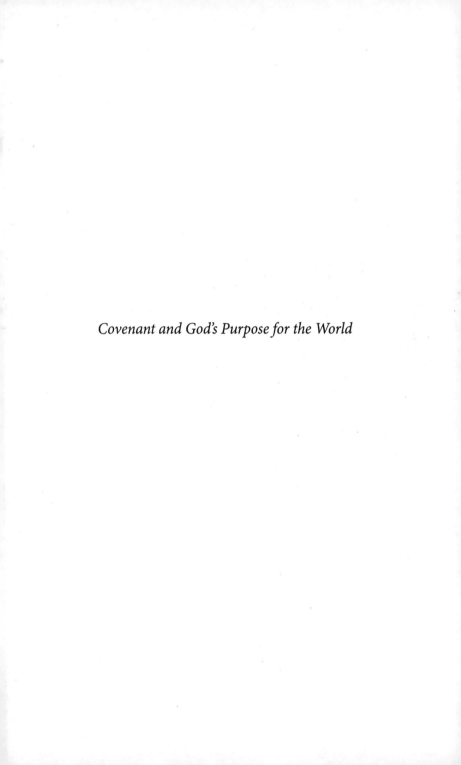

Covenant and God's Purpose for the World

Covenant and God's Purpose for the World

Thomas R. Schreiner

Dane C. Ortlund and Miles V. Van Pelt,
series editors

WHEATON, ILLINOIS

Trade paperback ISBN: 978-1-4335-4999-1
ePub ISBN: 978-1-4335-5002-7
PDF ISBN: 978-1-4335-5000-3
Mobipocket ISBN: 978-1-4335-5001-0

Library of Congress Cataloging-in-Publication Data

Names: Schreiner, Thomas R., author.
Title: Covenant and God's purpose for the world / Thomas R. Schreiner.
Description: Wheaton : Crossway, 2017. | Series: Short studies in biblical theology | Includes bibliographical references and index.
Identifiers: LCCN 2016057671| ISBN 9781433549991 (tp) | ISBN 9781433550010 (mobi) | ISBN 9781433550027 (epub)
Subjects: LCSH: Covenant theology—Biblical teaching. | Covenants—Biblical teaching. | Kingdom of God. | Jesus Christ—Kingdom.
Classification: LCC BT155 .S37 2017 | DDC 231.7/6—dc23
LC record available at https://lccn.loc.gov/2016057671

Crossway is a publishing ministry of Good News Publishers.

BP		27	26	25	24	23	22	21	20	19	18	17
15	14	13	12	11	10	9	8	7	6	5	4	3	2	1

To my fellow elders at Clifton Baptist.
"How good and pleasant it is
when brothers dwell in unity!"
—Psalm 133:1

Contents

Introduction

Covenant is one of the most important words in the Bible since it introduces one of the central theological themes in Scripture. Some scholars have even argued that covenant is the center of Scripture, the theme that integrates the message of the entire Bible. I am not convinced that covenant is the center of Scripture. Indeed, the idea that the Scriptures have one center is probably mistaken. Still, we can rightly say that covenant is one of the most important notions in the Bible.

The Importance of Covenant

The many scholars who have made covenant their integrating motif or central theme demonstrate how crucial it is. Indeed, covenant has played a vital role in theology from the beginning. Early church fathers, such as Origen, Irenaeus, and Augustine, assigned covenant a significant place in their writings. Covenant also came to prominence among the Reformers and their successors. Johannes Oecolampadius (1482–1531), Johannes Cocceius (1609–1669), and Herman Witsius (1636–1708) advanced the importance of covenant in interpreting the Scriptures.

In the modern period the importance of covenant was set forth by a number of scholars, perhaps most notably by the great Old

Testament scholar Walther Eichrodt (1890–1978). More recently, the landmark book by Peter Gentry and Stephen Wellum, *Kingdom through Covenant*, which uses covenant as a framework or a substructure to elucidate the storyline of the Bible, has been published.[1] At the same time, systematic theologians in the Reformed tradition, such as Michael Horton, have made the covenant an organizing motif in their dogmatic work.

Although such an approach is surely illuminating at a number of levels, it isn't necessary to insist that covenant is *the central* theme of biblical theology or *the key* for doing systematics. Even if one disagrees with those claims, we can say without exaggeration that we can't truly understand the Scriptures if we don't understand the covenants God made with his people. For even if covenant isn't the central theme of Scripture, it is still one of the central themes in biblical revelation. We can safely say, along with Gentry and Wellum, that the covenants are the backbone of the storyline of the Bible; they help us to unfold the biblical narrative. All careful readers of the Scriptures want to comprehend how the Bible fits together so that they can grasp the overarching narrative and theology of the Bible. We can't really apply the Scriptures wisely to our lives if we don't understand "the whole counsel of God" (Acts 20:27), and we can't grasp how the Scriptures fit together if we lack clarity about the covenants God made with his people.

If we have a nuanced understanding of covenants, we will gain clarity as to how the Old and New Testaments relate to each other. Such an endeavor is necessary since God didn't limit himself to one covenant, for we find in the Scriptures a covenant with Noah, a covenant with Abraham, a covenant with Israel, a covenant with David, and a new covenant. And many think God also made a covenant with Adam.

---

1. Peter J. Gentry and Stephen J. Wellum, *Kingdom through Covenant: A Biblical-Theological Understanding of the Covenants* (Wheaton, IL: Crossway, 2012).

To understand the Scriptures well, we need to understand how these covenants are interrelated, and we need to see how they advance the story of God's kingdom in the Scriptures. The covenants help us, then, to see the harmony and unity of the biblical message. They also play a vital role in tracing out the progress of redemptive history, which centers on the promise that God will bring redemption to the human race (Gen. 3:15).[2] Understanding the covenants is also essential for understanding the sacraments of baptism and the eucharist. Both of these signs are covenantal in nature and must be apprehended in that context.[3]

Definition of *Covenant*

Before launching into the study, we need to ask other vital questions. What is a covenant? What are we talking about when we use the word *covenant*, and how do we define it? Covenants can contain several elements, but here we want to look at what is required at minimum. *Covenant* can be defined as follows: a covenant is a chosen relationship in which two parties make binding promises to each other. Several things can be said about this definition.

First, a covenant is a relationship, and that sets it apart from a contract. Contracts also contain promises and obligations, but they are impersonal and nonrelational. Covenants stand apart from contracts because the promises are made in a relational context. We are not surprised to learn, then, that marriage in the Scriptures is described as a covenant (Prov. 2:17; Mal. 2:14). In marriage a husband and a wife choose to enter a covenant relationship, and they make binding promises to each other, pledging lifelong loyalty and faithfulness.

Second, a covenant is a chosen or elected relationship. Once

2. Genesis 3:15 isn't part of the covenant itself, but it does play a significant role in the unfolding narrative.

3. In this book, however, I will not explain how baptism and the Lord's Supper relate to the new covenant.

again, marriage serves as a good illustration. A husband and a wife choose to enter into the marriage covenant. By way of contrast, children and parents don't enter into a covenant with one another, for they are already bound together by their natural relationship, by their family bond. A covenant is a chosen relationship with defined responsibilities made with those who aren't already in a kinship relationship.

Third, a covenant relationship includes binding promises and obligations. We see this again in marriage, where spouses pledge themselves to each other. They promise to be faithful until death, living out the specific conditions and responsibilities in a covenant relationship. Each party in the relationship pledges to carry out the stipulations or the requirements of the covenant. Covenants, in other words, are mutual.

Still, not all covenants were alike in the ancient world. In some covenants a person with more authority made a covenant with those having less authority and power. Such was the case when a king made a relationship with his subjects. Readers of the Bible immediately think of God entering into covenant with human beings, for in this case we have a superior entering into covenant with an inferior. All covenants, then, aren't precisely the same, and we need to keep this in mind while studying the covenants in the Bible.

Examples of Covenants

We see a number of covenants between human beings in Scripture, and it should prove helpful to survey them briefly so that we can see how covenants operated in the biblical world. Both Abraham and Isaac had disputes with residents in Canaan over wells since water for flocks was in short supply. In one case, Abraham made a covenant with Abimelech over a well so that he could use the well without conflict (Gen. 21:24–32). Abraham and Abimelech made promises to one another and sealed their promises with an oath (v. 31). Abraham also gave seven lambs to Abimelech to serve as a witness of the covenant enacted. Isaac also disputed with the residents of Canaan over wells for his flocks (Gen. 26:14–33), so a covenant was made between Isaac and Abimelech,[4] which was sealed with an oath. They pledged not to harm each other and ratified the covenant with a meal. In both cases, we see that two parties entered into a formal relationship in enacting a covenant. They also made binding promises to each other, which were ratified with oaths. The covenant, then, was conditional, and each party promised to abide by its stipulations.

When Jacob fled from Laban accompanied by flocks, servants, and his wives (who were also Laban's daughters), Laban pursued Jacob in order to harm him (Gen. 31:17–55), but God appeared to Laban in a dream, warning him not to hurt Jacob in any way (v. 24). The meeting between Jacob and Laban was by no means friendly, as old family hurts and wrongs were voiced. Finally, they decided to conclude their complaints with a covenant (v. 44). They set up a heap of stones and a pillar, which served as a witness to the stipulations (vv. 45–48, 51–52). In the covenant, Jacob pledged to faithfully take care of Laban's daughters, and both Jacob and Laban promised to respect the boundary markers established by the stones and pillar (vv. 50–52). Neither would transgress the boundary and plunder the other. Jacob took an oath, and presumably Laban did as well, to observe the covenant stipulations (v. 53). The covenant was then sealed with a meal (v. 54). A formal relationship was thereby established between Jacob and Laban.

In the book of Joshua the Gibeonites deceived Israel and made a covenant with them to avoid being destroyed like the other inhabitants of Canaan (Josh. 9:3–27). Israel entered into the covenant

---

4. Abimelech is a dynastic name, so this person is not necessarily the same person Abraham dealt with.

relationship with the Gibeonites, pledging to let them live and promising peaceful relations. The covenant was ratified with an oath (v. 16). When Israel discovered that the Gibeonites had deceived them, some in Israel wanted to destroy them, but the Israelite leaders protested that they could not break the covenant since they had sworn oaths to the Gibeonites. If they transgressed the covenant stipulations, they would face the Lord's wrath (vv. 18–20).

The seriousness of the covenant is evidenced much later in Israel's history, when Saul violated its provisions by slaying the Gibeonites (2 Sam. 21:1). The Lord's anger was satisfied only after seven of Saul's descendants were put to death in exchange for the evil inflicted on the Gibeonites (vv. 2–9). Here we see all the elements of a covenant— a chosen relationship with promises ratified by an oath. We also see here that transgressing the covenant requirements led to judgment, which anticipates a theme we shall see later. Those who failed to keep covenant requirements were cursed.

Some scholars have said that covenants always presuppose an already existing relationship. The Gibeonite story shows that this is not the case, for Israel didn't have any relations with the Gibeonites before entering into a covenant with them. We can say the same thing about marriage in the ancient world. Typically, those who were married in Israel didn't "date" before getting married, and thus there wasn't a preexisting relationship. In other situations, of course, a relationship did preexist. We think of the covenants between Jacob and Laban, Abraham and Abimelech, and Jonathan and David. What we see, then, is that there was no distinctive pattern regarding the relationships between covenant parties, and thus it would be a mistake to conclude that a preexisting relationship was essential for establishing a covenant.

Jonathan and David made a covenant (1 Sam. 18:3–4; 20:8, 16–17; 22:8; 23:18). We don't expect Jonathan to support David, for

David was the greatest threat to Jonathan's succeeding his father as king. Nevertheless, we see Jonathan's love in his relationship with David. Jonathan gave to David his robe, armor, sword, bow, and belt as signs of his covenant with David. It is evident that Jonathan pledged to protect David's life, even from the hand of Jonathan's own father, Saul. Jonathan formalized the covenant by swearing his loyalty to David (20:17).[5]

Political alliances or covenants were apparently common. We read that the general Abner, who had aligned himself with Ish-bosheth, defected from Ish-bosheth and proposed to make a covenant with David so the latter could reign as king over all Israel (2 Sam. 3:12, 13, 21). So, too, the people of Hebron entered into a covenant with David and crowned him as their king (2 Sam. 5:3). King Solomon and King Hiram of Tyre also made a covenant with each other (1 Kings 5:12). King Asa of Judah made a covenant with Ben-hadad so that Ben-hadad would break his covenant with Baasha, king of Israel, and enter into a covenant with Asa instead (1 Kings 15:18–20; see also 1 Kings 20:34).[6] In every instance, those making a covenant entered a formal relationship in which promises were made.

The story of the covenant enacted in Jeremiah 34 is most interesting. The people of Jerusalem had made a covenant to set free all their Hebrew slaves (34:9–10). Unfortunately, the people changed their mind and took back their slaves (vv. 11–12), and thus they violated the covenant requirements they had promised to uphold. The covenant they transgressed was not merely a private one, for they had pledged before God, when he made his covenant with Israel, to free any Hebrew after six years of slavery (vv. 12–14; cf. Ex. 21:2; Deut. 15:12). The covenant to free Hebrew slaves was made

---

5. By way of contrast, see Psalm 55:20.

6. Sometimes it seems that the word *covenant* simply means a solemn agreement or vow. Job "made a covenant with my eyes" (Job 31:1), so that he would not see a virgin. Similarly, the Lord mocks the idea that human beings could make a covenant with Leviathan (Job 41:4).

in Yahweh's temple, and yet they repudiated what they had pledged to do (vv. 15–17).

Jeremiah then tells us something fascinating, for we learn more about the ritual that inaugurated the covenant (vv. 18–20). Israel ratified the covenant by cutting a calf in two and walking between the parts of the dead animal. This signified the curse that would come upon them if they broke the covenant—they would be sacrificed and slain for violating its provisions. This is often called a "self-maledictory oath," which means that one calls evil upon oneself for violating the provisions of the covenant.

Conclusion

We have seen that covenant is a major theme in the Scriptures, warranting an examination of its role in the biblical narrative. If we understand God's covenants, we will have a solid grasp of the storyline and theology of the Scriptures. We defined *covenant* as a chosen relationship in which two parties make binding promises to each other. Those binding promises are often accompanied by oaths, and there are often signs (the pillar and stones in the case of Jacob and Laban) and ceremonies (covenant meals) as well. We have also seen that not all covenants are accompanied by sacrifices, and thus sacrifices and the spilling of blood are not required to enter into a covenant. A preexisting relationship is not a prerequisite for establishing a covenant, as is evident in the case of Israel's covenant with the Gibeonites. Some covenants in Scripture are personal (Jacob and Laban, David and Jonathan); there are also political covenants (Asa and Ben-hadad, David and Judah), marriage covenants, and legal agreements within a nation (freeing of Hebrew slaves). In every instance, two parties enter a formal relationship in which they make promises to the other.

1

The Covenant of Creation

This chapter is perhaps the most controversial in the book, for the chapter title says there is a covenant at creation, but we don't find the word *covenant* anywhere in Genesis 1–3. Am I guilty of imposing something on the biblical text that isn't there? The great Presbyterian theologian John Murray said it would be better to speak of an Adamic administration rather than a covenant with Adam. According to Murray, covenants are always redemptive and given to human beings who have sinned. Therefore, it doesn't fit to speak of a covenant with Adam and Eve, in Murray's view, since they were without sin when God created them.

It is understandable why doubts arise about a creation covenant since the term *covenant* is lacking. When we add to this the unique circumstances of Adam and Eve in the garden, further ammunition is added to the argument that *covenant* is not quite the right term. A word should be said about terminology before going further. Those who believe that there was a covenant with Adam use different terms to label it, such as "covenant of life," "covenant of nature," or "covenant of works." The same general idea is involved, whatever the terminology. I prefer "covenant of creation" because it fits with an overarching view of redemptive history, enabling us to see how this covenant integrates with other covenants. In other words, God inaugurated history with creation and will consummate it with the new creation, and thus the old creation anticipates and points forward to the new creation. Still, there is no need to linger on the matter of terminology since the vital issue is the nature of the covenant.

Evidence for a Creation Covenant

I argue that we indeed can identify God's relationship with Adam and Eve as a covenant, for the following reasons. First, the word *covenant* doesn't have to be present for a covenant to exist, contrary to an older word-study approach that today is rejected by virtually all scholars. Today most scholars recognize that the concept of covenant can be present without the actual word. We find a remarkable example of this in the Scriptures. God enters into a covenant with David in 2 Samuel 7 (see also 1 Chronicles 17), but the word *covenant* isn't used there to describe the promise the Lord made to David. Is it legitimate to identify God's promise to David's dynasty in 2 Samuel 7 as a covenant? Certainly, for subsequent biblical writers, in reflecting on God's promise to David, specifically call it a covenant (Ps. 89:3, 28, 34, 39; 132:12; Jer. 33:21). It is apparent, then, that the concept of covenant may be present when the word is entirely lacking.

Second, we have textual evidence for a covenant at creation, so the analogy to the covenant with David stands on even firmer footing. We read in Hosea 6:7, "But like Adam they transgressed the covenant; / there they dealt faithlessly with me." The interpretation is disputed, but a reference to a covenant with Adam is the most likely reading. Some say that the word "there" in the verse is a place rather than a person. Is *Adam* ever referred to as a place in the Old Testament? The answer is yes, for we read in Joshua 3:16 that the waters stood up in a heap at Adam, when Israel crossed the Jordan into the Land of Promise. Still, it is highly unlikely that Hosea has in mind the place called Adam. How do we decide whether Adam the place or Adam the person is intended? The answer rests on which of the two is more likely in Hosea's context. Remember that Hosea was talking about Israel's sin and transgression in referring to Adam, and a reference to the place Adam in Joshua 3:16 (the only time the place is mentioned in the Bible) has nothing to do with Israel's sin and transgression. Actually, the story in Joshua 3 is one of the great triumphs in Israel's history, where they crossed the Jordan and stood on the verge of conquering the Promised Land. Seeing a reference to the person Adam, on the other hand, makes perfect sense. Israel, like Adam, transgressed the covenant God made with them. What is striking here is that God describes the relationship with Adam as a covenant! As we shall see, Israel in a sense was a new Adam, and like the first Adam they violated God's covenant. In using the word "there," it may be that Hosea was referring to the garden where Adam spurned God's command, or alternatively perhaps he had Gilead in mind (v. 8). In either case, a reference to Adam is still intended.[1]

Third, we have good reasons to see a covenant at creation because the constituent elements of a covenant were present at creation. There were two partners: God and Adam/Eve. God as the covenant Lord gave stipulations or requirements, demanding that Adam and Eve refuse to eat from the "tree of the knowledge of good and evil" (Gen. 2:17; 3:3, 11). Furthermore, there were cursings and blessings for disobedience and obedience, which, as we shall see, were present in later covenants. The covenant was conditional: if Adam and Eve disobeyed, they would die (Gen. 2:17; 3:3), but if they obeyed they

---

1. Jeremiah 33:20, 25 refers to God's covenant with day and night, which could also be called a covenant with creation. Still, it isn't clear from this text that the covenant described here was also made with Adam and Eve. It seems that Jeremiah is playing with the word *covenant* and applying it to fixed regularity of the natural world.

would enjoy life with God. Speculation has arisen as to how long the covenant was meant to endure. Some speculate that it was intended to end, and it seems fair to infer that eventually God would withdraw the test and confirm that Adam and Eve had shown covenant loyalty. The other view, that the covenant was unending, is equally speculative, for is it really likely that the test would last forever?

Fourth, John Murray and some others say that covenants exist only in redemptive relationships, and since Adam and Eve hadn't sinned, they didn't need redemption, nor was a covenant necessary. Once again, the objection doesn't stand, for the notion that covenants exist only where there are redemptive relationships isn't borne out by the evidence. Indeed, we have already seen that all kinds of covenants are made when redemption isn't in view. Marriage is covenantal even though the marriage covenant isn't redemptive in nature (Prov. 2:17; Mal. 2:14). Many other covenants in Scripture weren't made in a redemptive context, such as the covenants between Jacob and Laban (Gen. 31:44–54), David and Jonathan (1 Sam. 18:3–4; 20:8, 16–17; 22:8; 23:18), Israel and the Gibeonites (Josh. 9:3–27), and Solomon and Hiram of Tyre (1 Kings 5:12). To sum up, covenants can exist apart from redemption, so the argument against a creation covenant on that basis isn't decisive.

Fifth, the parallel between Adam and Christ enunciated in Romans 5:12–19 and 1 Corinthians 15:21–22 supports a covenant of creation. Both Adam and Christ functioned as representatives of those who belong to them. They are covenant heads! Therefore, sin, death, and condemnation belong to all human beings by virtue of their covenant connection to Adam, and grace, righteousness, and life belong to all those united to Jesus Christ. The covenantal and representational role of Adam is clear in the biblical storyline.

Sixth, God's covenant with Noah was said to be "established" rather than "cut," which might well indicate that the Noahic covenant was a renewal of the covenant with Adam rather than something completely new (see Gen. 6:18; 9:9, 11, 17). The argument is that the phrase "establish a covenant" refers to the renewal of a covenant that has already been instituted, while "cut a covenant" indicates that a new covenant is being inaugurated. There are some exceptions to this lexical argument (e.g., Deut. 29:1; Ezek. 16:60, 62), but in most cases "establish a covenant" means a previous covenant is renewed. We should not rely on this lexical argument to defend the idea that the Noahic covenant was a renewal of the covenant with Adam, for there are other good reasons to think so, as we will see in chapter 2.

The Significance of Being Created in God's Image

God created Adam and Eve, placing them in the beautiful garden he had made, the garden where he walked among them so that they enjoyed fellowship with him. God made Adam and Eve in his image (Gen. 1:26), and scholars have long discussed what it means to be created in the image and likeness of God. Space is lacking here to explore the matter adequately, so I will restrict myself to a few observations. It is probable that the words *image* and *likeness* are synonyms, and thus the difference between the two words should not be pressed. In the ancient world an image (i.e., a statue) was set up to denote the rule of a king over a region. It doesn't follow; however, that *image* is equated with or limited to ruling.

Still, the emphasis in Genesis is on the call for Adam and Eve to rule the world as those made in the image of God. We read in Genesis 1:26 that they were created in God's image and after his likeness so that they would "have dominion over the fish of the sea and over the birds of the heavens and over the livestock and over all the earth and over every creeping thing that creeps on the earth." The focus on rule is evident as well from Genesis 1:28: "Be fruitful and multiply and fill the earth and subdue it, and have dominion over the fish of the sea and over the birds of the heavens and over every living thing that moves on the earth." We see the same notion in Genesis 2:15, where Adam and Eve are placed in the garden "to work it and keep it." In other words, God made Adam and Eve in his image so that they would govern the world on his behalf. They would serve as his vice-regents, managing and stewarding and caring for the world under God's lordship.

A close relationship exists between image and sonship. Genesis 5:3 says, "When Adam had lived 130 years, he fathered a son in his own likeness, after his image, and named him Seth." Seth was in the image and likeness of Adam because he was the son of Adam. So also in Egypt the king was said to be in the image of god because he was considered to be the son of god. Adam is also "the son of God" (Luke 3:38), and sonship designates a special and unique relationship to God. Adam and Eve were to exercise their rule as God's children, as those in fellowship with God. Their rule wasn't independent of God but was to be carried out in his presence and for his glory since he is the sovereign Creator (cf. 1 Cor. 11:7). Adam and Eve in their rule, then, were to represent God and reflect his likeness. By displaying his character and holiness, they would bring glory to God. Sons bring glory to their parents by living righteous and beautiful lives, and Adam and Eve would bring glory to God by living in accord with his character. Adam and Eve would show they were God's children by their righteousness.

Incidentally, the image of God was not lost after Adam and Eve fell into sin, even though it was marred. A number of texts clarify that all human beings are made in the image and likeness of God, even though sin has entered the world (Gen. 5:3; 9:6; James 3:9). Part of what it means to be a son is to be like one's father, so we aren't surprised to discover that full restoration of the image means that human beings come to know God (Col. 3:10), and all those who know God become righteous and holy (Eph. 4:24). Adam and Eve's being created in God's image and likeness was not just a functional matter, for they were created as God's sons and children to be like their Father so that they reflected God's love and character as they ruled the world on his behalf.

If we look forward in redemptive history, we see that human beings are restored to the purpose for which they were made when they are "conformed to the image" of God's Son (Rom. 8:29). Only those who belong to the last Adam, Jesus Christ, are restored to the purpose for which God created human beings as sons and daughters of God. Believers in Jesus Christ are being slowly transformed into the image of God (2 Cor. 3:18). They are being changed "from glory to glory" and will fully bear the image of Christ on the day of resurrection (1 Cor. 15:49). Then they will be like their firstborn brother, Jesus, and will no longer be stained or defiled by evil (Rom. 8:29).

Ruling as Priest-Kings

Adam and Eve were made in God's image to rule the world as God's servants and his sons. There is also evidence they were to function as priest-kings. They were to mediate God's blessing to the world as the king and queen of God's creation. The garden anticipates the tabernacle (Exodus 25–31) since God specially resided in the garden, as he later dwelt in the tabernacle. What made the garden so lovely was God's presence with Adam and Eve; it was a place where Adam and Eve enjoyed God's fellowship and love.

We see a number of connections between the garden and the tabernacle and subsequently the temple. (1) God was specially present in the garden and specially present in the tabernacle. (2) The cherubim guarded the garden (Gen. 3:24), and the cherubim hovered over the ark in the tabernacle (Ex. 25:18–22) and were also stitched into the curtains and veil of the tabernacle (Ex. 26:1, 31). (3) Both the garden and the tabernacle were entered from the east (Gen. 3:24; Num. 3:38. (4) The many-branched lampstand may symbolize the tree of life (Gen. 2:9; 3:22; Ex. 25:31–35), for light was often associated with life. (5) The verbs used in Genesis 2:15 are also used of the work of the Levites in the sanctuary (Num. 3:7–8; 18:5–6). Adam was to "work" and "keep" the garden, and the Levites were to "work" and "keep" the tabernacle. (6) A river flowed from Eden and watered and fructified the garden, and so too a river flowed from Ezekiel's temple and made salt water fresh so that trees bore fruit (Gen. 2:10; Ezek. 47:1–12). (7) Stones found in Eden, both gold and onyx, were also in the tabernacle (Gen. 2:11–12; Ex. 25:7, 11, 17, 31). (8) It is likely that both the garden and the tabernacle were on a mountain, which was sacred land in the ancient Near East. The Old Testament describes the temple as being on Mount Zion, and the garden was probably elevated, for the river divided and became four rivers and thereby watered the land. All this evidence supports the notion that Adam and Eve were to be priest-kings in the garden, exercising God's rule over the garden and mediating his blessing to the world while they depended upon him for everything.

The Test

The man and the woman, however, were not to exercise their priestly rule autonomously. They were ever subject to the will of God, and thus they were to rule under his lordship. The Lord showered his goodness upon them by placing them in an idyllic garden with verdant trees from which they were nourished, and the man and the woman were to reveal their submission to God's lordship by refusing to eat from "the tree of the knowledge of good and evil" (2:17). If they consumed the fruit, they would experience death. We have here both the condition of the covenant, and the curse that would come if the covenant was transgressed. It is clear from this account that Adam and Eve were called to perfect obedience. Partial obedience would not suffice; one transgression would lead to death. The covenantal requirement was clearly set forth, and the penalty for infringement was not hidden.

There was not only covenant cursing but also covenant blessing. If Adam and Eve obeyed, they would enjoy life. The "tree of life" (2:9; 3:22, 24) anticipated the final joy of human beings who know the Lord (cf. Rev. 22:2, 14, 19). It seems fair to conclude that if Adam and Eve had passed the test, God would have, at some point, confirmed them in righteousness. Such a matter is speculative since the narrative doesn't answer that question. Still, it seems sensible to think that if Adam and Eve had continued to obey, they would eventually have been confirmed in righteousness.

Since Adam and Eve disobeyed, the curses of the covenant came upon them. More specifically, they experienced the death that had been threatened—they were separated from fellowship with God. When we consider all of Scripture, it is clear that the implications of Adam's disobedience weren't limited to him and Eve. We see in Romans 5:12–19 and 1 Corinthians 15:21–22 that sin, death, and condemnation spread to all people because of Adam's sin. The curses of the covenant weren't limited to Adam and Eve alone; they had a universal impact.

After the fall we see immediately the monumental consequences of Adam's sin. Murder plagues the first family as Cain slays Abel (Gen. 4:8). Genesis 5 records the roll call of death in generation after generation, documenting the impact of Adam's sin on all those who succeeded him. When we come to the time of Noah, sin's triumph over humanity is indisputable. Adam had unleashed a monster into the world. Hence, the early chapters testify to Adam's representational and covenantal role, even if they don't articulate it in the same terms we find in Romans 5:12–19.

The Promise

In Genesis 3:15 we read:

> I will put enmity between you and the woman,
>> and between your offspring and her offspring;
> he shall bruise your head,
>> and you shall bruise his heel.

Genesis 3:15 isn't directly related to the covenant with Adam. Certainly Adam and Eve didn't deserve mercy after breaking the provisions of the covenant. Still, God promised that the offspring of the woman would crush the head of the Serpent, even though the Serpent would bruise the heel of the woman's offspring. This promise was ultimately fulfilled in Jesus Christ (Rom. 16:20), and thus the disobedience of Adam and Eve was not the end of the story. God didn't destroy humanity; he promised ultimate victory over the Serpent through the offspring of the woman. How that story plays out is the subject of subsequent chapters.

Conclusion

We have good reasons for seeing a covenant at creation. Even though the word *covenant* is lacking, the elements of a covenant relationship are present, and Hosea 6:7 supports the idea that the relationship with Adam and Eve was covenantal. The claim that all covenants are redemptive isn't borne out by the use of the term in the Scriptures, for the term is lacking in the inauguration of the Davidic covenant (2 Samuel 7). The elements of a covenant were also present at creation, for blessing was promised for obedience and cursing for disobedience.

Adam and Eve were made in God's image to rule the world on his behalf. They were to be priest-kings in God's creation as sons of God.

They were to represent God on earth and display his righteousness and holiness and goodness in the way they lived and exercised lordship over the garden. Their fall into sin plunged the human race into the abyss where death and sin reign. When we look at the biblical narrative as a whole, we see that Jesus Christ is the last Adam who grants righteousness and life to his people (Rom. 5:12–19; 1 Cor. 15:21–22). Adam as a covenant head brought misery and death to the world, but believers will reign in life (Rom. 5:17) through the last Adam, Jesus Christ.

2

The Covenant with Noah

The next covenant is labeled as the "covenant with Noah," but it could be called the "covenant of preservation" since God instituted it to preserve human beings from destruction. God pledged in this covenant that humanity will not be annihilated before the promise of Genesis 3:15 is realized. Human beings will not only experience judgment and death; many will enjoy the tree of life planted in the first garden (Rev. 2:7; 22:2, 14, 19). God's gracious purposes for human beings will not be frustrated.

The background for this covenant is set by the narrative that follows Adam and Eve's transgression of the creation covenant (Genesis 3). The world unraveled as sin enfolded humanity in its tentacles. Cain showed that he was the offspring of the Serpent (1 John 3:12; cf. John 8:44) by slaying Abel, the offspring of the woman (Gen. 4:8). Lamech's brutality, cynicism, and arrogance testify that evil was gaining the upper hand (Gen. 4:23–24). The roll call of death in Genesis 5 also verifies that sin and death had come to reign. However one interprets the story about the sons of God and the daughters of men in Genesis 6:1–4, all agree that evil was advancing by leaps and bounds.

The depth of evil in the human heart is revealed in Genesis 6:5: "The Lord saw that the wickedness of man was great in the earth, and that every intention of the thoughts of his heart was only evil continually." It is hard to imagine a more telling commentary on the impact of Adam's sin, for no room is left for optimism about the human condition. Evil had become a tsunami that had swept away all goodness: "*every* intention," "*only* evil," and "continually." The extent of evil was pervasive, for the earth had become defiled by human corruption and violence (Gen. 6:11–13).

God's response accords with his righteous and holy character. He regretted that he made human beings and was so grieved over their evil that he decided to destroy them, along with all creatures except for the fish of the sea (vv. 6–7, 13). No one finally triumphs over the Lord, and at the end of the day, evil cannot and will not win, and thus God's enemies are swept away in judgment. In Noah's day, God sent a flood as a cataclysm to destroy his enemies and to vindicate his holiness.

Noah as a New Adam

God's judgment on the world was comprehensive, but one man stood out as an exception. "Noah found favor in the eyes of the Lord" (Gen. 6:8), for he was "righteous," "blameless," and "walked with God" (v. 9). Hence, Noah and his family would not be destroyed in the impending cataclysm. God graciously spared Noah by instructing him to build an ark as a bulwark for him and his family when the flood arrived. Noah was spared because of his righteousness, as the narrative in Genesis and the later reflections in Ezekiel attest (Ezek. 14:14, 20). We learn later, however, that Noah walked with God by virtue of his faith (Heb. 11:7). Noah didn't earn or merit God's favor; he pleased God because of his faith, and his goodness testified to his trust in God.

Moses draws parallels between the new start with Noah and the initial creation of Adam and Eve, indicating that a fresh era had commenced, that there was something like a new creation after the flood. Noah, then, was a kind of new Adam, though the parallel doesn't stand at every point since Noah was a sinner, and Adam at creation was righteous and free from sin. Still, the parallels are quite striking in the portrayal of Noah as a kind of new Adam.

First, God's work of ordering and shaping the creation occurred when the earth was covered with water and chaos (Gen. 1:2). So too, after the flood the earth was inundated with water, and a new beginning took place when the water receded. Second, God created the birds, creeping things, and animals to flourish and multiply on earth (Gen. 1:20–21, 24–25). After the flood, the birds, creeping things, and animals again began to propagate on the earth (8:17–19). Third, God created the sun and the moon to distinguish the day from the night and to establish the seasons of the year (Gen. 1:14–18). After the flood, the regular pattern of the natural world resumed in "seedtime and harvest, cold and heat, summer and winter, day and night" (Gen. 8:22). Fourth, Adam and Eve were blessed by God and enjoined to be fruitful and multiply (Gen. 1:28). With Noah, the command was issued afresh; the flood didn't represent the abolition of human beings. Additionally, the injunction to be fruitful and multiply was issued anew, and God blessed Noah as he had blessed Adam and Eve (Gen. 9:1, 7).

Fifth, Adam and Eve were given dominion over the world (Gen. 1:26, 28; 2:14). They were to rule the world as God's vice-regents. God reinstated this rule in a fallen world and revealed that animals, birds, and fish are under the rule of human beings (Gen. 9:2). Sixth, God provided food for humans in giving them fruits and vegetables to eat (Gen. 1:29). In the new world after the flood, the provision of food was reiterated, though now that provision included the consumption of animals (Gen. 9:3). Seventh, we saw earlier that human beings are the crown of creation because they are made in the image of God (Gen. 1:26). We wonder if the image was lost after sin and death entered the world, but God teaches Noah that human beings retained God's image. They are still magnificent and wonderful despite being ravaged by sin (Gen. 9:6).

Eighth, as noted in chapter 1, the cutting of a covenant represented a new covenant, but the establishing of a covenant represented the renewal of a covenant already in place. If this distinction follows, the covenant with Noah reestablished the covenant made with Adam and Eve at creation (see Gen. 6:18; 9:11). Even if this particular argument isn't convincing, the first seven points demonstrate that Noah was a kind of new Adam. The proviso, of course, was that Noah lived in a fallen world, and because the world wasn't renewed, there was both continuity and discontinuity with Adam.

The Nature of the Covenant with Noah

The fundamental feature of the covenant with Noah was the promise to preserve the human race, which was signaled by God's protecting Noah and his family in the ark while the flood raged on earth (Gen. 6:18). As long as human life continues, the ground will never again be cursed as it was in the flood (Gen. 8:21). The regular seasons of winter, spring, summer, and fall will continue, and human life will not be extinguished (Gen. 8:21–22). The covenant wasn't made only with Noah but also applied to all living creatures and human beings (Gen. 9:9–10). The essential promise of the covenant follows: "I establish my covenant with you, that never again shall all flesh be cut off by the waters of the flood, and never again shall there be a flood to destroy the earth" (v. 11).

Many covenants have signs, and we are specifically told that a sign was attached to the covenant with Noah (v. 12). God set his bow in the clouds as a sign of the covenant, to remember his covenant with human beings (vv. 12–17). Obviously, this doesn't mean that God might forget the covenant without the bow; it means that the bow is an ongoing testimony to God's faithfulness to his covenant promise. The sign constitutes God's oath and promise that the covenant will not be withdrawn. Indeed, the covenant made here is "everlasting" (v. 16) and was meant "for all future generations" (v. 12; cf. Isa. 54:9). It was a universal covenant in that it was made with Noah and with "every living creature of all flesh" (Gen. 9:15). The universal character of the covenant is particularly important and so it is repeated twice more (vv. 16–17). The covenant doesn't promise universal salvation, but it does guarantee universal preservation. The bow, as the sign of the covenant, represents a weapon of war (cf. Gen. 48:22; Josh. 24:12; 1 Sam. 2:4). If God unleashed his bow and let it fly, then all humanity would be destroyed. The sign of the covenant is that God has withdrawn his bow. He has put his weapons of war down and will not wipe out the human race again.

At first glance we could possibly read the covenant as if it pledged only that the world would not be deluged again with water. Surely, the covenant does promise this. Is it possible, then, that the world will be destroyed another way? The answer is no, not before the consummation of redemptive history. In promising no future flood, God was pledging that human beings will be preserved until the end of history. No other natural disaster, such as an earthquake, tornado, hurricane, or fire, will destroy the entire world. God pledged that he will be merciful and faithful—the world will endure until his promises are fulfilled. The covenant with Noah, as Jeremiah puts it, certifies "the fixed order of heaven and earth" (Jer. 33:25). It ensures that "day and night" will come "at their appointed time" (v. 20). The created world isn't going to implode or go crazy; there will be stability and order so that life on earth is sustained. In other words, God will fulfill the promise of Genesis 3:15 before history concludes. The covenant with Noah is a creation covenant in that it guarantees the continuance of the world until the great events of redemptive history are consummated. The covenant, therefore, is not limited to a certain person or a particular people. It was made with all people everywhere.

This covenant, like the covenant with Adam, is a creation covenant; it relates to all of creation. This is not to say that it has nothing to do with redemption, for redemption can't occur without a created order. And God blessed Noah, as he did Adam and Eve, enjoining them to be fruitful and multiply (Gen. 1:28; 9:1). Redemption occurs when human beings multiply and rule the world under God's lordship and for his glory. Redemption takes place, then, in a creational context, so that the salvation promised is realized in this world. God, in giving the covenant sign, binds himself to his oath and assures humanity that he will be faithful in both creation and redemption. Still, the covenant with Noah isn't redemptive in and of itself, though it promises that the world will continue until God's purposes and redemption are achieved.

Why was the covenant with Noah needed? Why did the creation covenant need to be renewed? To answer, we need to return to the reason the flood occurred. We saw in Genesis 6:5 the depth and pervasiveness of human corruption. Every thought was only and continually evil; the world was filled with violence and hatred. As a result God judged the world with a flood and began anew with one man, Noah, who was, as we noted, a new Adam. The question, though, is whether the new start would make any difference.

When we look at the world as it is, we often wonder if it would help to start all over again. The story of Noah tells us that the human race had started again, but God was under no illusions as to what would happen. After Noah offered sacrifice and it pleased God, the Lord said, "I will never again curse the ground because of man, for the intention of man's heart is evil from his youth. Neither will I ever again strike down every living creature as I have done" (Gen. 8:21). The discerning reader recognizes there some words from Genesis 6:5. The fundamental nature of human beings hadn't changed since the flood. The intention of the heart was still defiled by evil. Starting over again wouldn't lead to Eden. The evil that plagued the world was evident in the fear that existed between creatures and human beings (Gen. 9:2), and human beings were then permitted to eat meat, though they must drain the blood (vv. 3–4). In a world red in tooth and claw, animals that kill human beings were to be killed (v. 5).

The covenant to preserve the world, then, wasn't grounded on human godliness and goodness. Instead, the continuity of the world is due to the mercy of God. He extends what is often called "common grace" in allowing human society to develop rather than destroying it. Isaiah 24:5 is likely a reference to the covenant with Noah, where the prophet mentions the "everlasting covenant." And we see in Isaiah's words that the cancer at the root of the human heart hadn't been exorcised. "The earth lies defiled under its inhabitants; / for they have transgressed the laws, / violated the statutes, / broken the everlasting covenant" (Isa. 24:5).

Some have argued that all God's covenants are a blend of unconditional and conditional elements. This observation is true of many of the covenants. It is difficult to see, however, how the word *conditional* plays any meaningful role when it comes to the Noahic covenant. There are some provisions and responsibilities required of human beings, as we shall see shortly. But there is no evidence that failure to carry out these provisions cancels the covenant pledge. God has assured humanity that the world will continue until the end of time, until the second coming of Jesus Christ.

Peter sees three great cataclysmic events: the creation of the world, the flood during Noah's generation, and the destruction of the world by fire when Jesus returns (2 Pet. 3:5–7). In the meantime, before Jesus comes, the world will continue with all its order and stability. This doesn't mean, of course, that there aren't hurricanes, tsunamis, and earthquakes. What the Noahic covenant teaches is that despite the disruptions in the natural order, the world will go on. Life will not be snuffed out altogether. Tragedies and disasters will occur, but the world and life in it will persist. In this sense, the covenant is unconditional.

Since the basic flaw with human beings wasn't remedied by the flood (Gen. 8:21), God instituted human government in the Noahic covenant to restrain evil. Such restraint is mandated in Genesis 9:6, where human society is called upon to punish with death those who take the lives of others without cause. The ground for the injunction is that human beings are made in the image of God. Since human beings are magnificent and awesome, those who murder them must pay the price. Human society, then, plays a role in God's common-grace administration in seeing that justice is meted out to those who pursue evil, particularly to those who take the life of another.

The New Beginning

Noah and his family constituted a new beginning. Noah, like Adam, was in a garden, and like Adam he sinned in the garden. He planted a vineyard, got drunk, and lay naked in his tent (Gen. 9:20–21). Ham dishonored Noah in his nakedness, and Ham's son Canaan was cursed for Ham's actions (vv. 22–25). The new beginning under Noah was much like the first beginning. In the case of Noah and his family, the sin residing in the human heart burst forth quickly. God promised to preserve the world, but the world after Noah obviously wasn't paradise. The new family (Noah's) had all the same problems as the old family (Adam's). Once again, a distinction is drawn between those who will be cursed and those who will be blessed (vv. 25–27), and so here the promise of redemption is implied (cf. Gen. 3:15).

As history passed, it seems that human beings had again reached a crisis point. They built the Tower of Babel to make a name for themselves (Gen. 11:4), a tower that reached to the heavens so that they could dispense with God and accomplish their own designs and purposes. The tower was significant in the eyes of human beings; it seemed to reach up to the heavens! But God mocked the effort of human beings, recognizing that their effort was puny. The tower was so small that God, so to speak, had to come down and take a look, for he couldn't see it from heaven (Gen. 11:5)!

God has promised to preserve the world and to sustain the human race, but the prospects for humanity looked dim since evil dominated human hearts. What is the answer to wickedness that plagues humanity? God's solution is provided in the covenant with Abraham, as we shall see in chapter 3.

Conclusion

The covenant with Noah is a covenant of preservation, signifying a new beginning for human beings and the continuance of life on earth until the time of the end. We saw in a number of ways that it repristinates the creation covenant. Despite the depth of human wickedness, human beings are still made in God's image, and God continues to bless them as they are fruitful and multiply on the earth. The flood testifies to what human beings deserve on account of wickedness, and it is a type of the final judgment to come (Matt. 24:36–41; 2 Pet. 2:5). The bow in the clouds, the sign of the covenant, testifies that God has withdrawn his weapons of war, that he will preserve the world until redemption is accomplished. God will not wipe out the world every few years and start over. The covenant with Noah doesn't provide redemption, but the preservation of creation is the context in which redemption will be realized.

3

The Covenant with Abraham

The covenant with Noah provided the conditions in which redemption could be accomplished, and God blessed Noah and his family by enjoining them to be fruitful and multiply. Nevertheless, evil still reigned after Noah's days, for as we saw in the story about the Tower of Babel (Gen. 11:1–9), the world continued in its downward spiral after the new start with Noah. The flood exposed the true nature of human beings and underscored the judgment deserved for forsaking God. The narrative provokes us to question where salvation will come from, especially since human beings haven't changed since the flood; a depth of corruption still inhabits the heart.

The solution didn't come from human beings but from the grace of God. The world was again spinning into greater evil and declining from the good purposes for which it was made. God, however, stepped in and called Abraham.[1] In a sense, the call of Abraham was one man against the world, since the rest of the world was opposed to

---

1. Abram's name isn't changed to Abraham until Genesis 17, but for the sake of simplicity I will identify him as Abraham throughout.

God. It is also important to see that Abraham's obedience wasn't the basis for his call, though he certainly did obey the commission given to him. Still, the foundation for Abraham's call and obedience was divine election. Nehemiah 9:7 says, "You are the LORD, the God who chose Abram and brought him out of Ur of the Chaldeans and gave him the name Abraham." The first move didn't belong to Abraham: God chose him and God brought him out of Ur. We see the same truth in Joshua 24:2–3:

> Thus says the LORD, the God of Israel, "Long ago, your fathers lived beyond the Euphrates, Terah, the father of Abraham and of Nahor; and they served other gods. Then I took your father Abraham from beyond the River and led him through all the land of Canaan, and made his offspring many."

Abraham was an idolater like the rest of his family, and Paul confirms Abraham's ungodliness in Romans 4:5. But God chose him and took him from Canaan. In the story of Abraham we see the truth that God justifies the ungodly. The fulfillment of the promise of Genesis 3:15, then, would come through Abraham's family, even though Abraham didn't deserve God's mercy.

Abraham was a kind of new Adam, representing a new beginning. Adam introduced curses to the world by virtue of his sin, and we find a roll call of five curses in Genesis up to this point in the story (3:14, 17; 4:11; 5:29; 9:25), but when Abraham comes on the scene, he receives a fivefold blessing (Gen. 12:1–3). The curses that descended upon the world through Adam would be reversed through Abraham and his family. Abraham obeyed God's call to leave his land and family to receive the blessings God promised. God originally blessed Adam and Eve (Gen. 1:28), but now the promise of blessing is channeled through Abraham.

The Three Promises Made to Abraham

When the promises were first made to Abraham in Genesis 12, the word *covenant* is absent. Given subsequent developments in chapters 15 and 17 where the word *covenant* appears, it is fitting to include the promises first enunciated in chapter 12 under the scope of the Abrahamic covenant.

The promises can be divided into three parts: offspring, land, and universal blessing. First, Abraham was promised offspring. In Genesis 12:2 the Lord says that Abraham would become "a great nation." The word *nation* indicates a people with an organized governmental structure, which we could call a "political entity." In other words, God promised Abraham a kingdom. As Genesis 18:18 says, Abraham would "become a great and mighty nation." This kingdom would be dramatically different from Babel, for it would be devoted to God and would govern for his glory and praise. The word *nation* also implies offspring, for Abraham couldn't be a great nation without offspring. We will examine Genesis 15 separately, but God promised Abraham there that his offspring would be as numerous as the stars (v. 5; cf. 13:16). And in Genesis 17 the promise was extended, for Abraham would "be the father of a multitude of nations" (v. 4). The connection to the kingdom is explicitly forged, for God told Abraham that "kings shall come from you" (v. 6). More specifically, kings would come from Abraham and Sarah (v. 16). Abraham's dramatic obedience in offering Isaac spurs the Lord to reaffirm his promise to Abraham. His offspring would increase "as the stars of heaven and as the sand that is on the seashore. And your offspring shall possess the gate of his enemies" (Gen. 22:17). Here we see both the numerous offspring and the political nature of the promise. The children of Abraham would multiply and rule on the earth by defeating their enemies.

The seed of the woman, in other words, would be the children of Abraham (Gen. 3:15), and they would rule over the Serpent and his offspring. We know from the New Testament that Jesus Christ is the offspring of Abraham (Gal. 3:16), the true heir of the promise. Hence, the promise of offspring and nation pointed toward the birth and rule of Jesus the Christ. The rule first vouchsafed to Adam would become a reality in Jesus Christ.

The promise of offspring was confirmed to Isaac (Gen. 26:4) and Jacob (Gen. 28:14; 35:11). The political nature of the promise was underscored in the promises to Jacob, for his offspring would "spread abroad to the west and to the east and to the north and to the south" (Gen. 28:14), implying that they would exercise power over other peoples. This is even clearer in Genesis 35:11, for there we are told, "A nation and a company of nations shall come from you, and kings shall come from your own body." The offspring are described as a nation, and once again the kingly nature of the rule is described.

As the narrative in Genesis unfolds, the promise of offspring was fulfilled slowly in the case of Abraham and Isaac. The story emphasizes that the offspring were a miracle, the consequence of God's grace. God would see to the fulfillment of the promise of children. When the book of Exodus opens, the covenant promise of offspring was coming to pass in remarkable ways. We read that Israel was "fruitful and increased greatly; they multiplied and grew exceedingly strong, so that the land was filled with them" (Ex. 1:7). Nevertheless, Israel was still enslaved in Egypt at the time, and thus the zenith of the fulfillment of the promise of offspring to Abraham was realized later during the reign of Solomon. "Judah and Israel were as many as the sand by the sea. They ate and drank and were happy" (1 Kings 4:20; cf. Gen. 22:17; 32:12). Subsequent to Solomon, however, Israel slid into sin and ended up in exile, both the northern and southern kingdoms. Nonetheless, God's promise of offspring was not withdrawn, as we shall see in our study of the Davidic covenant and the new covenant.

The second element of the promise was land. Abraham left his homeland at God's command with the promise that God would disclose to him a new land that would be his (Gen. 12:1). If Abraham was to some extent a new Adam, then the land was a kind of new Eden where the people of God would reside. After Abraham moved at God's direction, he was told that the land would be Canaan (Gen. 12:7; 13:14–17; 15:7, 16; 17:8; 22:17). The borders of the promise are also sketched in: Abraham's offspring would possess the land "from the river of Egypt to the great river, the river Euphrates" (Gen. 15:18). The land promise was confirmed to Isaac (Gen. 26:3) and Jacob (28:13–15; 35:12). God fulfilled the land promise by freeing Israel from Egypt (Ex. 3:13–17; 6:3–9). Under Joshua the land promise made to Abraham was fulfilled to a significant extent; Israel came into possession of Canaan, and God had fulfilled his covenant promises to Israel (Josh. 21:44–45; 24:13, 18–19).

The promise of land made to Abraham seems to have been fulfilled in its entirety in 1 Kings 4:21: "Solomon ruled over all the kingdoms from the Euphrates to the land of the Philistines and to the border of Egypt." During Solomon's reign Israel seemed to be on the cusp of becoming a blessing to all nations. But near the end of Solomon's reign things begin to go awry. Solomon, under the influence of his wives, turned toward the worship of idols, and a process began that led to the dissolution of all Israel. By 586 BC both Israel and Judah had been exiled from their land, and even after they returned from exile the glory days under Solomon weren't renewed. Israel remained under the thumb of foreign powers and struggled as a second- or even third-rate power. The promise of land seemed to be withdrawn, for Israel wasn't advancing but regressing. Still, the promise was not cancelled.

The third promise to Abraham was that through him all nations would be blessed (Gen. 12:3). The promise of universal blessing was confirmed to Abraham (Gen. 18:18; 22:18), Isaac (Gen. 26:4), and Jacob (Gen. 28:14). The promise picks up the words of blessing given to Adam and Eve (Gen. 1:28) and Noah (Gen. 9:1). The divine intention at creation will be realized. The promise of universal blessing isn't emphasized in the Pentateuch or in the Historical Books, though it surfaces here and there. We have a glimmer of what is to come in Ruth, and Solomon prays that foreigners will come to know the Lord's name (1 Kings 8:41–43). The theme of universal blessing is prominent in the Psalms (e.g., Pss. 22:27; 67:7; 96:7) and the Prophets (e.g., Isa. 2:1–4; 11:10; 12:4; 19:16–25; 42:6–7; 45:22; 49:6; 52:15; 55:4–5; Joel 2:28; Amos 9:11–12; Jonah 1:1–4:11; Mic. 4:1–5; Zeph. 3:9–10). Noteworthy here is that the covenant with Abraham was never focused solely on Israel; from the beginning there was concern that the entire world would experience blessing. If Abraham was a kind of new Adam in a kind of new Eden, then there was a desire to see this blessing extend to the entire world. Through Abraham the whole world would be reclaimed for the glory of God. The promise of Genesis 3:15 would reach the entire world through a child of Abraham, and the New Testament clearly teaches that this promise was realized in Jesus Christ (Gal. 3:16). Still, we need to examine the Davidic and new covenants to trace this theme in all its richness.

The Covenant in Genesis 15

As Genesis 15 opens, the Lord's promise of offspring contradicts Abraham's experience. God had said that Abraham would become a great nation, and yet he didn't have even a single child. Abraham wondered if that meant, after so many years of not having a child, that his servant Eliezer would be the heir of the promise. The Lord promised Abraham that the heir would not be his servant but his son (v. 4). In fact, he summoned Abraham to gaze at the night sky to count the stars (v. 5). Abraham's offspring would be as uncountable as the stars. Abraham could have responded with incredulity and scoffed at such an outlandish promise. We are told, though, that he "believed the LORD" and it was "counted to him as righteousness" (v. 6). Abraham's righteousness is ascribed not to his work *for* God but to his trust *in* God. Paul explains that Abraham's right relationship with God stemmed from his faith instead of his works (Rom. 4:1–25; Gal. 3:6–9). Furthermore, we should not think that this is the first time Abraham believed. Hebrews informs us that Abraham's migration from Ur to Canaan was animated by his faith (Heb. 11:8).

God reaffirmed the promise of offspring in Genesis 15 but clarified that the number of offspring would be more than Abraham could count. We have an indication here that the universal blessing would be realized through the countless children of Abraham. God then reminded Abraham of the promise of the land (Gen. 15:7), another promise that had not yet been fulfilled, so Abraham asked for assurance that he would truly receive it (v. 8). God made a covenant with Abraham to verify the promise of the land (vv. 18–21). The covenant was ratified with a ceremony. Various animals were cut in half and laid "over against the other" (v. 10).[2] As we noted earlier, walking between the cut-up parts of animals was a means of staking one's life on faithfully adhering to covenant terms.

We are reminded, then, of the significance of Abraham cutting up the animals and setting them over against one another. Remarkably, Abraham doesn't walk between the cut-up animals. Instead, we read that "a smoking fire pot and a flaming torch passed between these pieces" (Gen. 15:17). The smoke and fire represented God himself, for he appeared to Moses in a flaming fire in the bush (Ex. 3:2), and Mount Sinai was enveloped with smoke when the Lord descended

---

2. The birds weren't cut in half but laid over against one another.

(Ex. 19:18; cf. 20:18). The Lord also led his people with a pillar of cloud and of fire (Ex. 13:21).

Abraham and the Lord did not walk through the cut-up pieces together. The Lord alone passed through the animals, and hence the Lord called a curse down upon himself, pledging that he would annihilate himself if he failed to fulfill the promise of land to Abraham and his heirs. We see here the unconditional character of the covenant with Abraham. This was not a mutual pact in which God and Abraham played equal roles; God would certainly fulfill the covenant; he staked his own existence upon his promise. This is not to say that there weren't conditions for Abraham. There certainly were conditions, as we will soon see.

The Covenant in Genesis 17

Abraham and Sarah contrived to have a child to fulfill the promise of offspring, and the plan appears to have worked since Abraham and Hagar together had a child called Ishmael (Genesis 16). It becomes apparent in subsequent chapters that their plan was not in accord with God's intention. The child of promise was to come from Sarah and Abraham, and thus the promise would flow through Isaac, not Ishmael (Gen. 17:15–21). The "everlasting covenant" is with Isaac (17:19), so Isaac will be the heir rather than Ishmael (21:10). Abraham's offspring would be named through Isaac instead of Ishmael (21:12). The line of covenant blessing, then, is funneled through Isaac.

What is most fascinating in Genesis 17 is the emphasis on covenant. Some have said there is a separate and distinct covenant with Abraham here. Unlike the covenant established in Genesis 15, the covenant here had conditions: it required circumcision of all who wanted to be members of the covenant (17:9–14). Circumcision became the covenant sign, and those who refused the sign were to be excluded from membership. Circumcision signified dedication to God, showing consecration and devotion to him.

At the same time, Genesis 17 is where the names of Abraham and Sarah were changed. Abraham was promised that he would be the father of many nations. The rite of circumcision fits with this promise as well, for circumcision reminded Abraham and his descendants daily that the many nations to descend from him could not be ascribed to his virility but only to the grace of God.

Nevertheless, the covenant described in Genesis 17 should not be seen as a new and distinct covenant with Abraham. Instead, it is a further explanation and supplementation of the covenant that God had already made with him. We have the language of establishing a covenant, which as noted earlier often (though not always) designated the confirmation or renewal of a covenant already enacted (Gen. 17:7). Even more important are the promises of the covenant. Since the promises here are the same as those given in Genesis 12, it is quite unlikely that a new and distinct covenant was intended. Genesis 17 focuses on the many offspring Abraham would have, but such a promise had already been made in chapters 12 and 15. So, too, the promise of the land of Canaan is reaffirmed (17:8). It is difficult to believe that the covenant is a new one when the promises of the covenant are the same ones we find earlier.

The reaffirmation of earlier promises doesn't mean that there were no new features in the restatement of the covenant in Genesis 17. The emphasis on Abraham's being the "father of a multitude of nations" is distinct (vv. 4, 5). In addition, we also see that "kings" will come from Abraham (v. 6). The covenant is "everlasting" (vv. 7, 13), and the land will be an "everlasting possession" (v. 8). Furthermore, it is clarified that the covenant is with Isaac rather than Ishmael (vv. 15–21). God would establish his covenant with Isaac (v. 21), and the covenant with Isaac was to be "everlasting" (v. 19).

The conditions given in Genesis 17 are one of the fundamental reasons some see a distinct covenant here; the covenant in chapter 15 is unconditional. Certainly the emphasis in these two chapters is different, but a better solution is to see that the covenant with Abraham had both conditional and unconditional elements.

We also see a genealogical element in the covenant with Abraham. In that sense Ishmael is one of the sons of the covenant since he was circumcised (Gen. 17:9–14, 25–27). There is also a theocratic and nationalistic element. All sons of Abraham at birth are inducted into the covenant by circumcision. Paul's exposition in Romans 9 seems to bear out this point. One could be the physical and circumcised son of Abraham or Isaac and yet not belong to the elect people of God (vv. 6–13). In the covenant with Abraham one could be genealogically descended from Abraham by virtue of circumcision and yet still be uncircumcised in heart (cf. Deut. 10:16).

We will see that this genealogical element doesn't continue under the new covenant. In many respects the covenant with Abraham is fulfilled in the new covenant, but the covenants should not be collapsed together as if they are identical covenants, because there is discontinuity between the two as well. The new covenant differs from the Abrahamic covenant since the latter had nationalistic and genealogical elements, whereas the former is personal and spiritual. To say that the new covenant is personal is not to deny its corporate element. The point is that the new covenant promises regeneration to every covenant member.

The Role of Obedience in Abraham's Life

We saw in Genesis 15 that the covenant with Abraham was unconditional: God passed through the pieces alone! On the other hand, we see conditional elements in Genesis 17. Abraham had to be circumcised to be a covenant member. Furthermore, God summoned

Abraham to leave his land and promised him great blessings if he did so (Gen. 12:1–3). The initial command given to Abraham implies a condition—Abraham must obey and leave his homeland to receive what was promised.

Some scholars sharply distinguish "royal grant" covenants from "suzerain-vassal" covenants. In royal grant covenants a king calls a curse on himself if he doesn't fulfill the stipulations of the covenant. The king in this arrangement promises to protect his servant from harm. In a suzerain-vassal treaty the suzerain sovereignly imposes stipulations on his vassals. Some find great significance in the two kinds of covenants, saying that the royal grant covenants are unconditional and suzerain-vassal treaties are conditional. Therefore, it is argued, the Mosaic covenant is conditional as a suzerain-vassal treaty, while the covenant with Abraham is unconditional as a royal grant covenant. There is some truth to this analysis, but it is overly simplistic. For one thing, there are conditions in the covenant with Abraham as well, as we see.

Royal grant covenants and suzerain-vassal treaties were not as distinct as some make them to be. They are best viewed on a continuum rather than as outright opposites. In royal grant covenants servants had responsibilities, and in suzerain-vassal treaties the great king took care of his subjects. It is doubtful, then, that distinguishing between royal grant and suzerain-vassal covenants is a key for determining the nature of the covenant made. Furthermore, the textual evidence in the Scriptures to support the Abrahamic covenant as a royal grant covenant rather than a suzerain-vassal treaty isn't compelling or clearly specified in the text.

The emphasis on Abraham's obedience is quite remarkable in the narrative. We read these words in Genesis 18:19: "I have chosen him, that he may command his children and his household after him to keep the way of the LORD by doing righteousness and justice, so that the LORD may bring to Abraham what he has promised him." Clearly, the promises to Abraham depended upon the obedience of coming generations. Abraham and his children were to fulfill the role of Adam in the garden. They were to display God's glory by living righteous, just, and beautiful lives as his children. The conditional nature of the covenant is evident here, for the Lord tells Abraham that if his children fail to keep the Lord's way, they won't experience the blessings pledged.

The necessity of Abraham's obedience is also underscored in the sacrifice of Isaac, which is certainly the climactic account in Abraham's life.

> By myself I have sworn, declares the LORD, because you have done this and have not withheld your son, your only son, I will surely bless you, and I will surely multiply your offspring as the stars of heaven and as the sand that is on the seashore. And your offspring shall possess the gate of his enemies, and in your offspring shall all the nations of the earth be blessed, because you have obeyed my voice. (Gen. 22:16–18)

The promises made to Abraham are reiterated here. We saw initially that those promises were dependent upon Abraham's leaving his land. Here the promises of offspring and land belong to Abraham "because you have done this" (v. 16) and "because you have obeyed my voice" (v. 18). The text could scarcely be clearer—Abraham would receive the blessings because of his obedience. There is a sense in which the covenant with Abraham was both conditional and unconditional.

One other text mentions Abraham's obedience, when the promises made to Abraham were confirmed to Isaac:

> Sojourn in this land, and I will be with you and will bless you, for to you and to your offspring I will give all these lands, and

I will establish the oath that I swore to Abraham your father. I will multiply your offspring as the stars of heaven and will give to your offspring all these lands. And in your offspring all the nations of the earth shall be blessed, because Abraham obeyed my voice and kept my charge, my commandments, my statutes, and my laws. (Gen. 26:3–5)

There we see all three covenant promises: offspring, land, and universal blessing. Isaac as the son of the covenant would be the recipient of these blessings. The reason given for the reaffirmation of the promises was Abraham's obedience (cf. Neh. 9:7–8). Since Abraham kept God's commands and laws, the covenant promise would be given to Isaac as well.

It is evident from these texts on Abraham's obedience that the covenant can't simply be described as unconditional. The covenant also depended upon Abraham's obedience. But how does that fit with the fact that God alone passed between the cut-up animal pieces, thereby rendering the covenant unconditional? There is significant evidence that the covenant with Abraham is ultimately unconditional, in the sense that ultimately and finally the promises of the covenant will be fulfilled. For instance, (1) Moses asked the Lord not to destroy Israel after the golden calf episode, based on the covenant made with Abraham, Isaac, and Jacob (Ex. 32:13). (2) Moses based his prayer on the inviolability of God's promise to Abraham, suggesting that the covenant would certainly be fulfilled, that it had a permanent validity. (3) When Israel went into exile, the Lord would restore them to the land, based on his covenant with Isaac and Abraham (Lev. 26:42). Once again, we see that there is a sense in which the covenant with Abraham, even when the nation disobeyed, wasn't abrogated. The Lord would not abandon them forever.

We see the same sentiment in 2 Kings, as the author records

Israel's descent into sin, which eventually led to exile. Still, Israel would not be finally and fully forsaken. "But the LORD was gracious to them and had compassion on them, and he turned toward them, because of his covenant with Abraham, Isaac, and Jacob, and would not destroy them, nor has he cast them from his presence until now" (2 Kings 13:23). The covenant with Abraham wouldn't be cancelled because it was "everlasting" and sworn to him by an oath (1 Chron. 16:16–17; Ps. 105:9).

Similarly, Micah expected God to have mercy on Israel, to forgive her sins, and to fulfill his promises because of the promises sworn to Abraham (Mic. 7:14–20). When the New Testament commences, it is clear that there was still an expectation that the covenant with Abraham would be fulfilled. Both Mary and Zechariah saw the coming of Jesus as the fulfillment of the oath and covenant made with Abraham (Luke 1:55; 70–75). Despite all of Israel's sins, the covenant promises made to Abraham had not been withdrawn.

When we consider the conditional and unconditional elements of the Abrahamic covenant, the best approach is not to deny either truth; there is a sense in which the covenant is conditional and a sense in which it is unconditional. We must beware of suppressing some of the evidence, for in doing so, the richness and depth of the covenant will be lost. Still, some explanation must be given for how these two truths cohere.

We saw at the outset that the covenant with Abraham had its roots in the electing grace of God. God called Abraham and chose him as his own, even though Abraham was ungodly and an idolater. Hence, Abraham's obedience couldn't be the basis of his relationship with God. God's grace was the fountain and spring for the covenant.

It is also clear from Genesis 15 and many other texts that the covenant with Abraham was unconditional; there is a clear expectation that the covenant would be fulfilled at some point in the future, even if Israel was deeply unfaithful. At the end of the day, the covenant would be fulfilled since it depended upon God's mercy and faithfulness. We can put it this way: even though Genesis 3:15 isn't part of the Abrahamic covenant per se, the seed of the woman will most certainly triumph over the Serpent! (Gen. 3:15).

If the Abrahamic covenant is ultimately unconditional, how do we explain the conditions in the covenant? Clearly, covenant fulfillment depended on obedience, and the covenant was fulfilled in the case of Abraham because he did obey; he met the conditions of the covenant. Conversely, how does this accord with the unconditionality of the covenant? The best answer seems to be that God will see to it that the covenant is fulfilled. The covenant promises will most certainly be realized. We won't come to the end of history and discover that what God promised to Abraham never came to pass, for God stakes his own life on the fulfillment of the promises. At the same time, only those who believe and obey will experience the blessings of the covenant. Therefore, no one can presume on the blessings of the covenant, including Abraham's physical children, for they must believe and obey to receive those blessings.

John the Baptist warned that the biological children of Abraham won't receive the blessings of the covenant apart from obedience (Matt. 3:9–10). God's axe will cut down those who claim to be Abraham's children if they don't bear good fruit. Jesus said something quite similar: those who are truly Abraham's children demonstrate that they belong to Abraham if they love Jesus (John 8:39–40). Those who want to kill Jesus show that they aren't Abraham's true children. Paul emphasizes that the true children of Abraham are those who put their trust in Jesus Christ for salvation (Rom. 4:1–25; Gal. 3:6–9). Those who are the children of Abraham, those who enjoy the blessings of Abraham, don't rely on their works but put their faith in Jesus Christ.

Participation in the blessing and promises of Abraham belongs to those who believe and obey. No individual will enjoy the blessings of Abraham if he or she transgresses covenant requirements. In that sense, the promise is conditional. And yet the covenant is also unconditional; it will ultimately and finally be fulfilled in its entirety. God will see to it, by virtue of his grace, that some will keep what the covenant demands. As the Baptist says, God can raise up children for Abraham from stones (Matt. 3:9). God in his sovereignty guarantees that some will believe and obey; there will certainly be children of Abraham (those who put their faith in Jesus Christ). These will believe because God grants them faith (Eph. 2:8–9). The covenant is unconditional, for God will grant the grace for those who are his own to meet the covenant conditions.

We can go one step deeper. Ultimately, the only true child of Abraham is Jesus Christ (Gal. 3:16), for he is the only one who was completely obedient to God. Only Jesus Christ always and gladly did the will of God. Since Jesus is the true son of Abraham, the children of Abraham are those who belong to Jesus Christ. The covenant with Abraham is unconditional, for it is guaranteed by Jesus Christ, the obedient one. The covenant is unconditional because it depends upon God's word in Jesus Christ, which is always yes! God's promises are all fulfilled in Christ (2 Cor. 1:21–22), who is the God-man. As the true son of Abraham and the last Adam (and the true Israel and true King, for that matter), he obeyed God, and thus what God pledged to Abraham became a reality in Christ Jesus.

Conclusion

The covenant with Abraham plays a central role in the narrative. Abraham is a kind of new Adam who is promised a kind of new Eden (Canaan). The curses that descended upon the world through Adam would be undone through Abraham, as God promised Abraham offspring, land, and universal blessing. The offspring was Isaac, the children of Israel, and the Davidic king. Still, the promise finds its culmination in Jesus Christ as the true son of Abraham (Gal. 3:16). All those who belong to Jesus Christ by faith, whether they are Jews or Gentiles, are children of Abraham. The promise of land was fulfilled when Israel possessed Canaan under the leadership of Joshua and Solomon, yet Israel lost the land and went into exile because of sin. The promise of land was realized proleptically in the resurrection of Jesus Christ, for his resurrection represents the arrival of the new creation, and it will find its final fulfillment in the new creation—the new temple over which God and the Lamb will reign (Rev. 21:1–22:5). We see some instances of universal blessing in the Old Testament, but this promise to Abraham is fully and finally fulfilled in Jesus Christ through whom people from every tongue, tribe, people, and nation are included in Abraham's family.

The covenant with Abraham is both conditional and unconditional. On the one hand, it is conditioned upon Abraham's obedience, as we saw in a number of texts. Only those who are circumcised are part of the covenant! On the other hand, Genesis 15 clarifies that ultimately the covenant with Abraham is unconditional. God went through the cut-up animals alone, signifying that he will see to it that the covenant is realized. The tension between the unconditional and conditional elements of the covenant is resolved in Jesus Christ. As the obedient one, he is the mediator of God's covenant promises, and hence those who are united to Christ are the true children of Abraham. The covenant with Abraham has been fulfilled in the new covenant inaugurated by Jesus Christ, but we shouldn't make the mistake of thinking that the new covenant is simply an updating of the covenant with Abraham. There is a genealogical element in the covenant with Abraham (circumcision), which was left behind when the new covenant was inaugurated.

4

The Covenant with Israel

The next major covenant is with Israel and is called the "Mosaic covenant" or the "Sinai covenant." It is called the "Mosaic covenant" because Moses was the head of Israel when it was enacted. It is called the "Sinai covenant" because it was inaugurated and ratified at Mount Sinai.

A Gracious Covenant

The covenant with Israel is distinct, but some mistakenly separate it almost altogether from the covenant with Abraham and identify it as a legalistic covenant, as if in this case salvation is based on works. Such a separation doesn't do justice to the covenant with Israel. In particular, God rescued his people from Egyptian slavery and redeemed them in fulfillment of his covenant with Abraham, Isaac, and Jacob (Ex. 2:23–25). The close relationship between the covenant with Abraham and the covenant with Israel is apparent in Exodus 6:3–8. Yahweh's liberation of Israel and promise to bring them into the land fulfills his covenant with Abraham. The covenant formula, that Yahweh will be their God and they will be his people, will be established.

The same covenant relationship that Abraham, Isaac, and Jacob enjoyed with God would continue in the covenant Yahweh made with Israel. Indeed, when the Lord appears to Moses at the burning bush (Ex. 3:1–10), he emphasizes that he is the God of Abraham, Isaac, and Jacob so that Moses and Israel will understand that the covenant with Israel stands in continuity with the covenant with Abraham. We see the same theme in Deuteronomy 7:7–9 (see also Deut. 4:36–38; 9:5), where Moses explains to Israel that the Lord chose them to be his people and freed them from Egypt because of his sovereign election and because of the covenant he made with the patriarchs. The covenant with Israel and the covenant with Abraham aren't the same, but they stand in a close relationship and have a number of points of continuity.

The wording of Jeremiah 11:2–5 is perhaps the clearest indication of the continuity between the two covenants:

> "Hear the words of this covenant, and speak to the men of Judah and the inhabitants of Jerusalem. You shall say to them, Thus says the LORD, the God of Israel: Cursed be the man who does not hear the words of this covenant that I commanded your fathers when I brought them out of the land of Egypt, from the iron furnace, saying, Listen to my voice, and do all that I command you. So shall you be my people, and I will be your God, that I may confirm the oath that I swore to your fathers, to give them a land flowing with milk and honey, as at this day." Then I answered, "So be it, LORD."

Jeremiah in these words forges a link between the Abrahamic covenant and the covenant with Israel. God is the God of his people in both covenants, and God liberated Israel from Egypt and made a covenant with them to fulfill the promise of land made to Abraham. The heart of the covenant with Israel is that the Lord saves and protects his people. The tie between the two covenants is evident, for the promises of the covenant with Abraham are secured as Israel keeps the stipulations of the covenant at Sinai.

Another piece of evidence confirms that the covenant with Israel is gracious and not legalistic. Before God established his covenant with Israel, he redeemed them from slavery in Egypt and adopted Israel as his people; specifically, he adopted them as his son (Ex. 4:22–23), freeing them to be his people and he their God. The gracious nature of the covenant is underscored in Exodus 19–24. Before the covenant stipulations are given, the Lord reminds Israel of the grace he had shown them. He had judged the Egyptians and "bore" Israel "on eagles' wings and brought [them] to [himself]" (Ex. 19:4). The Lord doesn't begin with a demand that Israel observe these commands in order to be his people. Quite the contrary. Israel had done nothing to deserve the Lord's favor, and yet he rescued them from slavery, and only after he had bestowed such grace and mercy did he give them commands.

We see the same pattern in Exodus 20, the famous chapter where the Ten Words or the Ten Commandments are recorded. Before giving any of the commands, Yahweh says, "I am the LORD your God, who brought you out of the land of Egypt, out of the house of slavery" (Ex. 20:2). Before the covenant stipulations are declared, the Lord's covenant mercy is rehearsed. The God who calls for covenant loyalty in keeping his commands is the God who showered his love on Israel by freeing them from slavery. His grace and mercy precede and undergird his demands.

Suzerain-Vassal Parallels

It has often been observed that the Lord's covenant with Israel follows the pattern of suzerain-vassal treaties, which were very common in the ancient Near East from 1400 to 1200 BC. Many scholars see a parallel between the suzerain-vassal treaties and the covenant structure in Exodus and Deuteronomy. The great king enacts a covenant with his vassals, promising to protect and guard them, while the vassals are obligated to serve the sovereign by abiding by the covenant stipulations. There are various ways of identifying the elements of the treaty, but here I will focus on five elements.

Preamble	The sovereign identifies himself
Historical Prologue	The basis of the covenant is articulated in the sovereign's deliverance of the vassal, and the sovereign promises to provide for the vassal
Covenant Stipulations	The obligations are incumbent on the vassal
Covenant Blessings and Cursings	The benefits of keeping the covenant are rehearsed, and the liabilities of transgressing the covenant are also recorded
Deposit Treaty	The treaty is put in respective temples and read periodically, witnessing to the covenant

In the Old Testament, the sovereign is identified as Yahweh, and he enters a covenant with Israel after delivering them from Egypt, promising to be Israel's God and protector. The covenant pattern, then, features the grace of God! The covenant stipulations are found in various places, especially Exodus 20–23 and Deuteronomy 12–26. Israel must abide by these regulations to show their covenant loyalty to Yahweh. The blessings and cursings of the covenant are detailed in Leviticus 26 and Deuteronomy 26–28. If Israel keeps the covenant stipulations, they will experience prosperity and joy, but if they violate them, then curses and judgment will follow. Witness to the covenant is given through two tablets, which are deposited in the temple or ark (Ex. 25:16; 40:20; Deut. 10:2, 5; 1 Kings 8:9; 2 Chron. 5:10).

A Renewed Covenant and Covenant Lawsuits

Interestingly, Moses refers to a covenant at Moab in addition to the covenant made at Sinai (Deut. 29:1). Some understand this to be a new and distinct covenant. It makes more sense, though, to see this as a covenant renewal, since the requirements aren't different from those in the covenant enacted at Sinai. At Moab Moses renewed the covenant with a new generation, with the generation that was about to enter the Promised Land. Even though the covenant at Moab was not a new one, the verb *cut* is used. In other words, we can't base whether a covenant is new or renewed solely on the words *cut* and *establish*. Other evidence must also be adduced to make a determination.

We see the same phenomenon in Joshua 24. After possessing the land, Joshua rehearsed with the people the Lord's mercy in the time of Abraham, in the exodus, and in the possession of the land. He then asked them whether they chose to serve the Lord or other gods. Israel pledged to serve Yahweh. On that basis Joshua cut a covenant with them (Josh. 24:25). The rules and regulations of the covenant were set forth, and a stone was erected as a witness to the covenant (Josh. 24:25–27). Once again, here at Shechem, a covenant was being renewed rather than inaugurated. Joshua renewed the covenant ratified at Sinai with the people, and they pledged anew to abide by its stipulations.

The prophets denounced Israel because the nation violated the provisions of the covenant. Indeed, the prophets brought a case against Israel because they had broken the covenant with Yahweh. In other words, the prophets brought covenant lawsuits against God's people. We see this, for instance, in Hosea 4 where the prophet says that the Lord has a "controversy," i.e., a lawsuit against his people (v. 1). It is evident that Israel had violated the Ten Commandments, for they had failed to keep the first and greatest commandment of love and faithfulness to their covenant suzerain (Ex. 20:3; Deut. 6:5; Hos. 4:1). Israel's transgression of the covenant is also apparent in Hosea 4:2, where Hosea draws on the Ten Commandments without quoting them, complaining that "there is swearing, lying, murder, stealing, and committing adultery; they break all bounds, and bloodshed follows bloodshed." We see a similar covenant lawsuit in Micah 6. The Lord calls upon the mountains and the hills to hear his case, his indictment, against his people. The Lord had only done good for his people by freeing them from slavery in Egypt and promising to provide their every need (vv. 3–6). But Israel forsook the justice, mercy, and kindness required by the law; they refused to walk humbly with God (v. 8).

Many other texts in the Prophets fit this pattern, even if lawsuit language isn't used. Jeremiah 11 is a fitting example. Jeremiah reminds Judah of the covenant Yahweh had made with them. The covenant, however, proclaims a curse upon those who don't obey its provisions (Jer. 11:3). Judah turned away from the Lord's voice, failing to heed and obey his commands (v. 8). Both Judah and Israel devoted themselves to other gods and broke the covenant (v. 10). As a consequence, they would experience the curses of the covenant (v. 11). Elsewhere Jeremiah summarizes the reason the Lord will pour out his judgment on his people: "Because they have forsaken the covenant of the Lord their God and worshiped other gods and served them" (Jer. 22:9).

We see, then, that Israel renewed and repledged its loyalty to Yahweh a number of times. Such a state of affairs is clearly present in King Josiah's reign in Judah (640–609 BC). Josiah was one of the last kings in Judah, and the country was headed toward disaster. The people had violated the stipulations of the covenant in dramatic and shocking ways. The prophets had declared that the curses of the covenant were imminent because of Judah's disobedience. Josiah, upon unearthing the Book of the Covenant, had the words of the covenant read in the temple (2 Kings 24:2). As a consequence, "the king stood by the pillar and made a covenant before the Lord, to walk after the

LORD and to keep his commandments and his testimonies and his statutes with all his heart and all his soul, to perform the words of this covenant that were written in this book. And all the people joined in the covenant" (2 Kings 23:3). We see again here the word *cut* used for Josiah's renewing the Sinai covenant.

Blood and Sacrifices

The formal inauguration of the covenant is detailed in Exodus 24. Yahweh declared to Moses all his rules and commands, and these commands are described as the "Book of the Covenant," which Moses read to the people (v. 7). Israel responded to these stipulations by pledging to keep and observe them (v. 7). In other words, Israel promised to be a faithful covenant partner. The covenant was inaugurated with blood sacrifices. Part of the blood was thrown on the altar, presumably to purify the altar (v. 6). The blood was also thrown on the people, for as sinners Israel needed to be cleansed by blood before they could enter into covenant with the Lord (v. 8). The importance of blood is signified in the words, "Behold the blood of the covenant that the LORD has made with you in accordance with all these words" (v. 8). Israel wasn't qualified and worthy to enter into a covenant with Yahweh apart from blood, since they were defiled.

We also see the graciousness of the covenant and the need for atonement in the sacrifices that were offered for the cleansing of sin. These sacrifices are recorded in Leviticus 1–7 and reach their climax in Leviticus 16, which was the Day of Atonement on which all of Israel's sins were forgiven. The covenant, then, provided a means by which Israel could maintain fellowship with God, though defiance, deliberate sin which rejected the Lord's authority, could not be forgiven (Num. 15:30). Israel's covenant fellowship with God was not dependent on perfect obedience, since sacrifices could be offered for covenant violations. The covenant was sealed with a meal celebrated by Moses and the leading men in Israel (Ex. 24:9–11). Again we see a covenant meal featured in the enacting of a covenant, as we saw in the case of Isaac and Abimelech (Gen. 26:30) and Jacob and Laban (Gen. 31:54).

The Ten Commandments and the Sabbath as the Sign of the Covenant

We have also seen that it is typical for covenants to be marked by particular signs. In the case of the covenant with Noah, there was the bow in the clouds. Abraham's covenant with the Lord was signified by circumcision. The obligations of the covenant with Israel are summarized in the Ten Commandments (Ex. 20:3–17; Deut. 15:7–21). These commands commence with the central matter for Israel's life—the people must be devoted to Yahweh and to Yahweh alone. They must not give their allegiance to any other god, and they signify such by worshiping Yahweh alone, by refusing to make images of Yahweh or any other god, and by always honoring his name. In addition, Israel was to honor Yahweh by keeping the commands he gave them: they will honor their parents and refrain from murder, adultery, stealing, and lying, and will not covet or desire anything Yahweh has forbidden. The other covenant stipulations were really an expansion of these ten words or ten commands.

In the midst of these obligations we find the sign for the covenant with Israel: the Sabbath. The Sabbath's role as a covenant sign is indicated by its length—it is the longest commandment (Ex. 20:8–11; Deut. 5:12–16)—and its centrality in the listing of the commandments. The injunction to observe the Sabbath is communicated in more depth and with more words than any of the other commandments. We have no doubt that the Sabbath is a sign of the covenant since it is repeated twice (Ex. 31:13, 17). Moses emphasizes that the Sabbath is permanent for Israel "throughout your generations"

(Ex. 31:13, 16). It is "a sign forever" (v. 17), signifying the "covenant forever" (v. 16).

Israel's Call and Commission

If we think further about how the covenant with Israel relates to previous covenants, it is clearly quite different from the covenant with Noah. The covenant isn't made with everyone in the world but with the people of Israel. Israel is the covenant people of the Lord, the holy and elect people of Yahweh (Deut. 7:7–8). They are marked out as the children of Abraham. So just as Abraham was, in some respects, a new Adam, so too Israel is a new Adam. The blessing for the whole world will come through Israel. Israel is also specially designated as God's son and firstborn (Ex. 4:22–23); they are to represent God just as sons represent their father, and they represent him by living righteous and holy lives. The parallel with Adam before the fall into sin does not stand at every point. Israel was sinful and thus needed forgiveness for transgressions. Still, as the son of God, Israel (like Adam) was to live under God's authority and to display to the rest of the world the joy and blessing of living under God's rule.

Israel also inherited the land of Canaan, the land originally promised to Abraham, Isaac, and Jacob. In some ways, the land of Canaan functioned as a new Eden, a new garden where God was to manifest his rule over his people. Once again, we must note the discontinuity, for sin had entered the world and with it thorns and thistles (Gen. 3:17–19). Still, Israel was called upon to live as the people of God in the land he had given so that the world could see that Yahweh was supreme in every arena of Israel's life.

Israel, as the people of the Lord, was summoned to be "a kingdom of priests and a holy nation" (Ex. 19:6), mediating God's blessing to the world. Some understand this to mean that Israel had a mandate to go to all nations and proclaim the name of Yahweh. More likely,

Israel as a nation, as a people governed by the Lord, were to show the nations God's character by the way they lived under Yahweh's lordship. Their way of life would attract others to the Lord as they lived in humble submission to their great sovereign. Such a reading fits with the uniqueness of the covenant made with Israel, for the stipulations in the covenant, the laws, contained many requirements that separated Israel from other nations. For instance, many foods eaten by other nations were off-limits for Israel (Lev. 11:1–44). Furthermore, the sign of the covenant—the Sabbath—set Israel apart from other nations. Israel was called to be a distinct people, consecrated to the Lord. Their holy life would demonstrate their covenant commitment to Yahweh and serve as a light to the nations.

Covenant Stipulations and Covenant Obsolescence

Every covenant has stipulations and requirements. It is evident, though, that the Noahic covenant will endure even if the stipulations are violated. We have also seen in the Abrahamic covenant God's pledge that the covenant will most certainly be fulfilled despite its conditions. The covenant with Israel is quite different, for we don't find any promise of ultimate fulfillment. Indeed, as we shall see when we discuss the new covenant, the covenant with Israel has a built-in obsolescence. It was not intended to last forever. One reason for its temporary nature is the focus on Israel as a nation. The covenant with Israel was theocratic, established to distinguish them from all other nations and peoples. Said another way, the covenant with Israel had both a political and a religious dimension. Under the old covenant, the people of God were almost exclusively limited to Israel. They had a specific role in showing the world what it looked like to live under God's lordship as his son.

God warned Israel that they would experience the curses of the covenant if they didn't faithfully obey him (Lev. 26:14–44).

Deut. 27:15–26; 28:15–69). Indeed, Israel's disloyalty to their covenant king was sufficient enough to warrant a new covenant (Jer. 31:31–34), one in which God's people would be enabled to do his will. Israel experienced the curse of exile because they failed to do what the covenant at Sinai demanded.

Remarkably, the Mosaic covenant was blighted with pessimism from the outset. God hadn't granted Israel the ability to understand, see, and hear his word (Deut. 29:4). The curses of the covenant are much longer than the blessings in both Leviticus 26 and Deuteronomy 26–28, suggesting that they would certainly become a reality. In some instances, the certainty of the curses is assumed. We read in Deuteronomy 28:45, "All these curses shall come upon you and pursue you and overtake you till you are destroyed." The eventual experience of the curse is also apparent in Deuteronomy 30:1–3:

> When all these things come upon you, the blessing and the curse, which I have set before you, and you call them to mind among all the nations where the LORD your God has driven you, and return to the LORD your God, you and your children, and obey his voice in all that I command you today, with all your heart and with all your soul, then the LORD your God will restore your fortunes and have mercy on you.

The final word is optimistic, for the Lord will again have mercy on Israel (the new covenant!), but before the restoration would come exile and estrangement from the Lord.

Israel's treachery in the future is woven into the last chapters in Deuteronomy:

> Behold, you are about to lie down with your fathers. Then this people will rise and whore after the foreign gods among them in the land that they are entering, and they will forsake

me and break my covenant that I have made with them. Then my anger will be kindled against them in that day, and I will forsake them and hide my face from them, and they will be devoured. And many evils and troubles will come upon them. (31:16–17)

Moses also says in the same vein, "For I know that after my death you will surely act corruptly and turn aside from the way that I have commanded you. And in the days to come evil will befall you, because you will do what is evil in the sight of the LORD, provoking him to anger through the work of your hands" (Deut. 31:29). Similarly, the song of Moses in Deuteronomy 32 was composed to testify to Israel's future unfaithfulness. The Mosaic covenant was a gracious covenant, but the Lord didn't provide Israel with the moral ability to keep its requirements.

Interestingly, Joshua says something very similar when the covenant is renewed in Joshua 24. We might think that Joshua would have been optimistic about Israel's future since they had just conquered the land Yahweh had promised them. Instead, Joshua is skeptical about Israel's obedience, saying, "You are not able to serve the LORD, for he is a holy God. He is a jealous God; he will not forgive your transgressions or your sins. If you forsake the LORD and serve foreign gods, then he will turn and do you harm and consume you, after having done you good" (Josh. 24:19–20). Joshua here provides a forecast of Israel's history, since both the northern and southern kingdoms end up in exile for violating the covenant.

The weakness of the old covenant is borne out in Israel's history, and Paul testifies to the law's inadequacy as well: "The law came in to increase the trespass" (Rom. 5:20). We find a similar sentiment in Galatians 3:19, where Paul says that the law "was added because of transgressions." The context in Galatians makes clear that the law did not contain sin but fostered it. Israel was "held captive under the law, imprisoned until the coming faith would be revealed" (Gal. 3:23). Indeed, the law could not produce life, for instead of begetting obedience, it sparked rebellion and transgression. The old covenant was gracious, since God entered into it because of his mercy and delivered Israel even though they didn't deserve it. Still, the covenant pattern is "do this and live" (cf. Lev. 18:5; Rom. 10:5; Gal. 3:12). Israel failed to keep what the law demanded, and hence they were expelled from the land. If Israel didn't keep what the covenant required, they would "break my covenant" (Lev. 26:15; cf. Josh. 23:16).

Second Kings 17 rehearses why the northern kingdom went into exile, and the author emphasizes that they were punished because they broke their covenant with the Lord (2 Kings 17:15, 35, 38). When we look at the verses in context, it is plain that the covenant was broken because Israel violated its commands. The next chapter explains why Israel went into exile: "They did not obey the voice of the LORD their God but transgressed his covenant, even all that Moses the servant of the LORD commanded. They neither listened nor obeyed" (2 Kings 18:12).

As we come to the time of the prophets, the prospects for the fulfillment of the Abrahamic covenant seem bleak. Still, God always keeps his word, and the covenant with Abraham is fulfilled in the covenant with David and the new covenant. We see in Leviticus that the covenant promise is not withdrawn when Israel goes into exile, but the covenant referenced there is the one made with Abraham and Jacob (Lev. 26:42–45). So too, as Israel is hurtling into exile because of sin, the narrator pauses to underscore the fact that ultimately God's covenant with his people won't be broken: "But the LORD was gracious to them and had compassion on them, and he turned toward them, because of his covenant with Abraham, Isaac, and Jacob, and would not destroy them, nor has he cast them from his presence until now" (2 Kings 13:23). Israel broke the covenant made at Sinai, but the old covenant, the covenant made with Israel, was not God's last and final word. God's final word for his people is not judgment but mercy.

Conclusion

The covenant with Israel was gracious, for the Lord freed his people from Egyptian slavery. In some ways, it was an extension of the covenant with Abraham and Adam, for Israel was called as God's son and as a kingdom of priests to display the righteousness of the Lord to the world as they kept the covenant stipulations. The covenant with Israel was patterned after suzerain-vassal treaties in the ancient Near East. Blessings were promised for obedience and curses for disobedience. Israel was called as a theocracy to live under Yahweh's lordship, and that demanded the submission of every member of the nation, for he had entered into covenant with the entire nation.

We see in the history of Israel that they failed to abide by the covenant stipulations, summarized in the Ten Commandments, and thus they were sent into exile. The prophets declared in covenant lawsuits, which detailed Israel's violation of the covenant, that judgment was coming. Jeremiah and others, however, also prophesied a new covenant (Jer. 31:31–34), one in which the law would be inscribed on the heart. The covenant with Israel had a built-in obsolescence and focused on Israel as a nation; it did not transform the heart of those who heard the covenant demands. The prophets promised that a new day was coming, a new covenant would be realized, and thus there would be a new exodus, a new David, and a new creation.

5

The Covenant with David

Adam and Eve were called as priest-kings and as those made in the image of God to rule the world as God's vice-regents. They were to do so under God's lordship, but they rebelled against God and brought misery and death instead. God promised to reclaim the world through a child of Abraham. Through Abraham's offspring there would be worldwide blessing, and God would rule in the land of Canaan. When we come to the covenant with David, Israel was living under the Sinai covenant and hoping in the promises made to Abraham. King David and his sons would represent Israel, and the nation would be blessed through their obedience to Yahweh and their reign over the people. Their righteous rule would display to the world what it meant to live in the land under Yahweh. Hence, the covenant with David would bring about the promised blessings anticipated in the creation covenant, and the blessings promised in the covenants with Israel and Abraham would be realized. We are getting ahead of the story, however, so we need to back up and set the scene.

Inauguration of the Covenant

The covenant with David is established in 2 Samuel 7. Saul was appointed as the first king of Israel, but Saul was rejected as king because of his failure to trust in and obey the Lord. Two incidents in particular stand out. When Saul was commissioned by Samuel to annihilate the Amalekites, he failed to carry out all that the Lord commanded, saving the best of the animals and sparing Agag as king (1 Samuel 15). Second, on the eve of his fateful battle with the Philistines, Saul consulted with a necromancer to try to discern the future (1 Samuel 28). No one can represent Yahweh if he refuses to obey him! David, on the other hand, after being anointed by Samuel as king (1 Samuel 16), stands out for his trust in and obedience to the Lord. The remainder of the narrative in 1 Samuel demonstrates his confidence in God, whether he fought Goliath or the Philistines or fled from Saul.

The words of Hannah's song are the theme of David's life (1 Sam. 2:1–10). The Lord exalted the humble David and humiliated proud Saul; "he brings down . . . and raises up" (1 Sam. 2:6). Yahweh "[gives] strength to his king and [exalts] the horn of his anointed" (1 Sam. 2:10). We see the same theme in the song at the close of 2 Samuel (chap. 22). The songs of Hannah and David constitute the framework of 1–2 Samuel, which are really one book. David praised the Lord because he "delivered him from the hand of all his enemies, and from the hand of Saul" (2 Sam. 22:1). The Lord delivered David because he "kept the ways of the LORD and [had] not wickedly departed from my God" (2 Sam. 22:22).

The context and establishment of the covenant with David is set forth in 2 Samuel 7 and 1 Chronicles 17. David desired to build a house for the Lord, which pleased the Lord. Still, David had to beware of thinking that he could do anything for the Lord, as if God would be dependent upon David for a great temple. Actually, David was dependent on God for everything, for God was the one who took David from shepherding sheep and appointed him as the leader of Israel. Also, the Lord does not need a house to reside in; he was content to live in the tabernacle, and he transcends any house that could be built for the sake of his name. Nevertheless, a temple would be built, not by David but by Solomon, since David engaged in frequent wars.

The most astonishing feature of the story is that Yahweh promised to build David a house. David desired to build a house for the Lord, but the Lord countered by saying that he would build a house for David. We have a wordplay on the *house* here, for David wanted to build a house (the temple) for the Lord, but the Lord countered by promising David an everlasting house (i.e., an eternal dynasty). The Lord promised to establish his kingdom forever (2 Sam. 7:13), which means that he would never withdraw his faithful love from David's house (v. 15). David is promised, "Your house and your kingdom shall be made sure forever before me. Your throne shall be established forever" (v. 16; cf. v. 26).

Remarkably, the word *covenant* is absent in 2 Samuel 7, and there is no covenant sign or covenant meal. But there is a covenant just the same, which is confirmed in other texts. Even in context, the covenantal nature of what God pledged to David is clear: his dynasty and kingdom will never end. This is another way of saying that the promise to Abraham of universal blessing will be realized through a son of David. A Davidic king will be the means by which the promises of land, offspring, and worldwide blessing will be realized.

The King in the Pentateuch

There were intimations all along that the offspring of Abraham would be a king, for Abraham was promised that "kings shall come from

you" (Gen. 17:6; cf. 17:16), and the promise is confirmed to Jacob—
"kings shall come from your own body" (Gen. 35:11). We also learn
in Genesis 49:8–10 that the ruler among Israel will come from Judah.
"The scepter shall not depart from Judah, nor the ruler's staff from
between his feet, until tribute comes to him; and to him shall be the
obedience of the peoples" (Gen. 49:10). Most interesting here is that
the inclusion of other peoples will come through obedience to a ruler
from Judah. We have an early hint that the worldwide blessing promised to Abraham will come through a king. In Numbers 24:17–19
we see that a ruler from Jacob will destroy God's enemies and have
worldwide dominion. The promise of a king, then, is fulfilled in the
narrative in the rise of David and his dynasty.

A Conditional and Unconditional Covenant

The covenant with David has conditions and stipulations. We see
this clearly in 2 Samuel 7:14, which refers to Solomon, who will suc-
ceed David: "When he commits iniquity, I will discipline him with
the rod of men, with the stripes of the sons of men." The dynasty
won't be removed from David's house, and the covenant will finally
be fulfilled, but individual kings who transgress will not experience
blessing. They will be reproved and disciplined and even removed
if they stray from God's commands. This is quite similar to the covenant with Abraham, for there too we saw that the covenant would
ultimately be fulfilled, and yet those who disobey will not receive the
covenant blessings. The promises and blessings of the covenant are
realized only by those who obey the Lord.

We could say, then, that David is a new Adam and the true
Israel, the true son of Abraham, and that he is promised a descendant through whom all of God's promises will be secured. The
promise of Genesis 3:15 will reach its final fulfillment through one
of David's offspring.

If we had any doubt about whether the promise to David was a covenant, it is removed in Psalms 89 and 132. There we are told specifically that God made a covenant with David (Ps. 89:3, 28, 34, 39; 132:12). What bothers the psalmist in Psalm 89 is that the promises made to David seem to be withdrawn (vv. 39–51), and such a state of affairs doesn't fit with the permanence of the Davidic covenant (v. 4). "My steadfast love I will keep for him forever, / and my covenant will stand firm for him. I will establish his offspring forever / and his throne as the days of the heavens" (vv. 28–29). The psalmist recognizes that the covenant has clear conditions: "If his children forsake my law / and do not walk according to my rules, / if they violate my statutes / and do not keep my commandments, / then I will punish their transgression with the rod / and their iniquity with stripes" (vv. 30–32). No king who departs from the Torah will experience blessing. In that sense the covenant is conditional.

We see the same condition in Psalm 132: "If your sons keep my covenant / and my testimonies that I shall teach them, / their sons also forever / shall sit on your throne" (v. 12). Ultimately, however, the covenant is unconditional. After noting the conditions of the covenant, we read these crucial words in Psalm 89:

> I will not remove from him my steadfast love
>> or be false to my faithfulness.
> I will not violate my covenant
>> or alter the word that went forth from my lips.
> Once for all I have sworn by my holiness;
>> I will not lie to David.
> His offspring shall endure forever,
>> his throne as long as the sun before me.
> Like the moon it shall be established forever,
>> a faithful witness in the skies. (vv. 33–37)

God's promise that David would have a son sitting on the throne will not be revoked, although any king who turns away from God will be disciplined.

How do we resolve the tension between the conditional and unconditional statements in the covenant with David? The answer is that God will certainly fulfill his covenant, but the fulfillment will be realized only with an obedient king. After Israel disobeyed so dramatically and was exiled, the hope of a future king wasn't abandoned. We see in 1–2 Kings that the nation goes as the king goes. If the king obeyed, the nation prospered, but if the king transgressed, the nation declined. Exile and the loss of political power do not mean that the promise was withdrawn, though they do signify that the promise won't be fulfilled by means of kings who don't keep the covenant stipulations.

We should note the connection between the covenant with David and the covenant with Israel. The kings were judged (just as the nation was) for failing to keep the prescriptions of the covenant. Still, the covenant will ultimately be fulfilled through the obedient Son—Jesus, the Christ. The conditional and unconditional elements of the covenant are resolved in his person.

The Role of Psalm 72

Psalm 72 plays a vital role in helping us understand the relationship between the covenant with Abraham and the covenant with David. The psalm is clearly messianic, and the psalmist prays that the Lord will endow the king, God's royal son, with justice and strength to bestow blessing on the people. Particularly striking is the universal blessing and dominion anticipated here, for the psalmist is convinced that his prayer will be answered in accord with the Lord's covenants with Abraham and David. Verses 8–11 are remarkable, and the reference is to the Davidic king:

> May he have dominion from sea to sea,
>> and from the River to the ends of the earth!
> May desert tribes bow down before him,
>> and his enemies lick the dust!
> May the kings of Tarshish and of the coastlands
>> render him tribute;
> may the kings of Sheba and Seba
>> bring gifts!
> May all kings fall down before him,
>> all nations serve him!

Clearly, the promise made to Abraham of universal blessing will be fulfilled in the king, and the enemies licking the dust also alludes to victory over the Serpent, which supports the notion that the covenant with Abraham fulfills the promise enunciated in Genesis 3:15 (cf. Num. 24:17; Ps. 89:10, 23). The allusion to the universal blessing promised to Abraham (Gen. 12:3, etc.) is unmistakable in Psalm 72:17: "May people be blessed in him, / all nations call him blessed!" Clearly, the promise of worldwide blessing given to Abraham will be fulfilled through a son of David. The Davidic covenant is organically related to the covenant with Abraham, and a son of David will be the means by which the promises made to Abraham will come to pass.

The Davidic Promise in Israel's History and the Prophets

The history of Israel seems to contradict the promise. The nation ended up in exile under foreign rulers, and even in the Second Temple period we don't see any Jewish ruler from David's line exercising governing authority. Even as the kingship was dissolving because the kings were violating Yahweh's covenant, the covenant with David was irrevocable. Thus we read, "Yet the LORD was not willing to destroy the house of David, because of the covenant that he had made with

David, and since he had promised to give a lamp to him and to his sons forever" (2 Chron. 21:7).

The prophets also looked forward to the day when a new David would come. Isaiah prophesies that the promise will be fulfilled:

> For to us a child is born,
>> to us a son is given;
> and the government shall be upon his shoulder,
>> and his name shall be called
> Wonderful Counselor, Mighty God,
>> Everlasting Father, Prince of Peace.
> Of the increase of his government and of peace
>> there will be no end,
> on the throne of David and over his kingdom,
>> to establish it and to uphold it
> with justice and with righteousness
>> from this time forth and forevermore.
> The zeal of the LORD of hosts will do this. (Isa. 9:6–7;
>> cf. 16:5).

The coming Davidic king will be the true son of Adam, the true Israel, and will fulfill what all the previous Davidic kings were intended to be. The rule over creation first given to Adam will be realized in the government of this son. The justice and righteousness that mark human life under the rule of God will be on display through this king.

We see a similar prophecy in Jeremiah about the king:

> Behold, the days are coming, declares the LORD, when I will raise up for David a righteous Branch, and he shall reign as king and deal wisely, and shall execute justice and righteousness in the land. In his days Judah will be saved, and Israel

will dwell securely. And this is the name by which he will be called: "The LORD is our righteousness." (Jer. 23:5–6; cf. 30:9; 33:15–16)

The hopes for human flourishing and a just and righteous rule will come to fruition in a Davidic king. Despite the disappointment of exile and the fact that Israel's hopes seem to be crushed forever, Jeremiah reaffirms that "David shall never lack a man to sit on the throne of the house of Israel" (Jer. 33:17). The unconditional character of the covenant is evident, for God's promise to David can no more be broken than God's covenant with day and night (Jer. 33:20–21)—a son of David will reign! The sin of Israel's kings is not the last word.

Ezekiel also affirms the rule of a Davidic king. "And I will set up over them one shepherd, my servant David, and he shall feed them: he shall feed them and be their shepherd. And I, the LORD, will be their God, and my servant David shall be prince among them. I am the LORD; I have spoken" (Ezek. 34:23–24). The rule of David won't be temporary, for he "shall be their prince forever" (Ezek. 37:25). The same hope for a Davidic king also burns in Hosea (3:5), and Amos promises that "the booth of David" that had fallen into ruin and disrepair will be rebuilt (Amos 9:11). Similarly, Zechariah looks forward to a day when David's house will receive mercy (Zech. 12:10–13:1). These promises for Davidic rule are conjoined with Israel's rebirth so that ancient hopes for love and justice are revived.

The Fulfillment of the Davidic Covenant in the New Testament

The New Testament proclaims that the covenant with David is fulfilled in Jesus of Nazareth; he is the anointed one, the Christ. Both Matthew and Mark identify Jesus as the Christ in the first verse of their Gospels. They don't leave their readers in the dark about who Jesus is. The importance of Jesus's being the Christ is evident in the Synoptic Gospels, for one of the climactic points in the narrative is when Jesus asks the disciples about his identity and Peter proclaims that he is the Christ (Matt. 16:13–16; Mark 8:27–30; Luke 9:18–20), which means that he is the anointed one, the Davidic Messiah.

Another central moment arrived when Jesus was on trial and the high priest demanded to know whether he was the Christ, the Son of God (Matt. 26:63–66; Mark 14:61–64; Luke 22:67–71). Jesus's affirmative answer led to the charge of blasphemy, and he was crucified for claiming to be the Christ and God's Son. The messiahship of Jesus is equally important in John's Gospel, for when John articulates his purpose for writing, he tells the reader that he wrote so that they would believe that Jesus is the Christ and the Son of God (John 20:30–31).

We could devote much space to demonstrate from the Gospels that Jesus was considered to be the Messiah, the Son of David. What is clear is that the Gospel writers believed that Jesus fulfilled the covenant promise made to David (cf. Matt. 9:27; 15:22; 20:30–31; 21:9, 15; Mark 10:47–48; 11:10; Luke 1:27; 2:4; 18:38–39). We read in Luke 1:32–33, "He will be great and will be called the Son of the Most High. And the Lord God will give to him the throne of his father David, and he will reign over the house of Jacob forever, and of his kingdom there will be no end." Also, Zechariah praises God for the birth of Jesus, declaring that the Lord "has raised up a horn of salvation for us in the house of his servant David" (Luke 1:69).

We should note that Jesus's messianic status also fulfills the covenant with Abraham, for in the birth of Jesus God has "[shown] the mercy promised to our fathers" and has "[remembered] his holy covenant, the oath that he swore to our father Abraham" (Luke 1:72–73). We see here that the two covenants are organically related. Jesus is the true offspring of Abraham, and the promises of land and universal blessing will be realized in him.

The Davidic covenant will certainly be fulfilled, but the fulfillment will occur through an obedient king. Jesus as the son of David also stands out by virtue of his obedience to the Father. David, with all of his strengths, failed egregiously when he committed adultery with Bathsheba and murdered Uriah. Solomon departed from the Lord at the end of his life by turning toward idols. Jesus by way of contrast was the obedient son and thus was the true and perfect Adam, the true Israel, the true son of Abraham, and the true David. When Satan tempted him in the wilderness, he did not cease from trusting in or obeying the Lord, in contrast to Israel's experience in the wilderness (cf. Matt. 4:1–11; Luke 4:1–13). Jesus came as a servant and devoted his life to the Lord (Matt. 20:28; Mark 10:45). He did nothing on his own initiative but followed the initiative of the Father (John 5:19), insisting that he hadn't committed any sin (John 8:46). Instead, he committed his life to honoring and glorifying the Father (John 8:49; 17:4). Both elements of the Davidic covenant are realized in Jesus Christ. God fulfilled his unbreakable promise to David, and Jesus obeyed all the covenant stipulations.

In the book of Acts Jesus is heralded as the Christ for Israel and for all the world. Peter proclaims on the day of Pentecost, "Let all the house of Israel therefore know for certain that God has made him both Lord and Christ, this Jesus whom you crucified" (Acts 2:36). Jesus was the Christ during his earthly ministry, but after his resurrection he was exalted and crowned as Lord and Christ. A new stage of redemptive history has arrived since Jesus is the crucified, risen, and exalted Lord. The promise to David has been fulfilled, and Jesus as the son of David, as the Christ of the Lord, now reigns at God's right hand over the entire world. Jesus clearly interprets Psalm 110 this way (see Matt. 22:41–46). David's son and descendant is also

David's Lord! The epistle to the Hebrews picks up this same idea. Jesus, in fulfillment of Psalm 110, has now sat down (after his atoning sacrifice and resurrection) at God's right hand (Heb. 1:3; 8:1; 10:12; 12:2). He rules as a priest-king over the cosmos. He rules as the Davidic king until God places all enemies under his feet (1 Cor. 15:25). Jesus as the descendant of David is now by virtue of his resurrection also crowned as Lord (Rom. 1:3–4).

The promise of Davidic rule is even now being fulfilled since Jesus is ruling and reigning. Of course, there is a day when his reign will be not only inaugurated but also consummated, for every enemy will be utterly destroyed (1 Cor. 15:26). The new creation is coming (Rev. 21:1–22:5), where God and the Lamb will reign forever. In that day the promise to David will be fulfilled in its entirety since every enemy will be routed and Jesus will reign as Lord and Christ forever and ever (Rev. 11:15–19).

We have gotten ahead of ourselves a bit, for it is important to observe that the early church, after Jesus's ministry, proclaimed him as the Christ. We see this clearly with the apostles in the young days of the church, when they were still ministering in Jerusalem. "Every day, in the temple and from house to house, they did not cease teaching and preaching that the Christ is Jesus" (Acts 5:42). Or when Philip went to Samaria, he "proclaimed to them the Christ" (Acts 8:5). The Samaritans responded eagerly to Philip's preaching "when they believed Philip as he preached good news about the kingdom of God and the name of Jesus Christ" (Acts 8:12). Upon Paul's conversion, he began to proclaim the gospel in Damascus "by proving that Jesus was the Christ" (Acts 9:22). Peter instructed Cornelius and his friends, telling them that "Jesus Christ" is "Lord of all" (Acts 10:36). So, too, when Paul arrived at Thessalonica he preached, "This Jesus, whom I proclaim to you, is the Christ" (Acts 17:3), and the same pattern was followed in Corinth (Acts 18:5). Apollos is commended for the power of his preaching, and he demonstrated from the Scriptures "that the Christ was Jesus" (Acts 18:28). Other texts could be adduced, but the point is clear. The early Christians believed that the covenant with David was fulfilled in Jesus of Nazareth. He is regularly identified as the Christ, showing that he is the anointed one of David.

Sometimes scholars say that Paul wasn't interested in Jesus's being the son of David, arguing that "Christ" lost its significance as a title in his writings. But this is very improbable, for Paul was a Jew and believed that the Scriptures were fulfilled in Jesus. Indeed, in Romans 1:2–3 Paul emphasizes that Jesus is the Davidic Messiah according to the Scriptures, showing that such a teaching was important to him (cf. 2 Tim. 2:8). He probably didn't emphasize Jesus's Davidic roots more often in the Epistles because his letters were written to specific situations, typically to churches he had planted and evangelized, at which time he would have argued for Jesus as Messiah in his oral proclamation of the gospel. Acts 13 represents the typical sermon Paul preached in synagogues, and it is evident there that Paul argued from the Scriptures that Jesus was the Messiah. Apparently, the churches he planted didn't dispute or question that fact.

We need to remember that Paul's letters were not systematic treatises; they were crafted to react to the situations in the churches he planted. It is most interesting, then, that Paul emphasizes that Jesus is the son of David and the Messiah at the outset of his letter to the Romans (Rom. 1:3), a church he hadn't established. In this case, Jesus's messianic status is a matter he sets forth at the outset, which suggests that the issue is important to Paul.

That brings us back to what was said earlier. It is quite unlikely that Paul used the title "Christ" as a throw-away word. The messianic significance of the appellation wasn't lost on him, and it almost certainly retained significance in his thinking. Paul uses the word

Christ, the phrase *Christ Jesus*, or *Jesus Christ* approximately 375 times, which shows the importance of the title in his thinking.

We have already seen that the title "Christ" is important in Hebrews, which is attested by fifteen uses of the title. Remarkably, Peter uses the term nineteen times in his first letter and seven times in his second epistle. It is striking that Jesus Christ is regularly identified as Lord in the second letter of Peter, for that title emphasizes his rule, showing again that the promise of a Davidic king is fulfilled in Jesus's lordship over all.

Many other passages could be cited to support the same notion. One of the most important is found in 1 Peter 3:21–22, where Jesus at his resurrection is exalted to "the right hand of God, with angels, authorities, and powers having been subjected to him." Similarly, Jude identifies Jesus Christ as Lord in four instances (Jude 4, 17, 21, 25). John in his epistles emphasizes that one must confess that the historical Jesus is the Christ (1 John 2:22–23; 4:2; 5:6; 2 John 7). Those who deny that the Christ has come in the flesh of Jesus do not belong to God.

Finally, the book of Revelation also trumpets that Jesus is the Christ. The seven-sealed book, which is the key to human history and the redemption of the human race, is off-limits to all creation, except to Jesus Christ (Revelation 5). He is the only one "worthy" to open the sealed book, showing that he is the key and center of redemptive history. Jesus's victory, however, can't be separated from his messianic identity. Better, it is rooted in his messianic identity. He conquers as "the Lion of the tribe of Judah, the Root of David" (v. 5). The rule over the world promised in Genesis 3:15 to the offspring of the woman, which is then narrowed to the offspring of Abraham, and which is then narrowed to a son of David, finds its fulfillment in Jesus Christ. He is the Lion who conquers as the slain Lamb (Rev. 5:5–6; cf. 22:16). In Revelation the title "Christ" appears especially where there is an emphasis on ruling and reigning. Jesus is "the ruler of kings on earth" and "the firstborn of the dead" (Rev. 1:5). The commission to rule over the world given in the covenant to Adam is fulfilled in the rule and reign of Jesus Christ. His authority as the Christ is manifested in the expulsion of Satan from heaven (Rev. 12:10) and in the reign of the saints (Rev. 20:4, 6). And as the Christ and the Lord "he shall reign forever and ever" (Rev. 11:15).

Conclusion

The covenant with David stands in continuity with previous covenants. The rule over the world originally given to Adam would be realized through a Davidic king. The promises of offspring, land, and blessing given to Abraham would be secured through the Davidic ruler. In a similar way the blessings promised in the Mosaic covenant would come to fruition under faithful Davidic kings, but if they strayed from the Lord, then the curses would come. Though some of the kings in Judah were godly, ultimately the curses of the covenant came upon the people and their king, and the defection of the kings from the Lord played a decisive role.

The covenant with David had both conditional and unconditional elements. Since the covenant was conditional, kings who departed from the Lord were judged, and after the exile we no longer see Davidic kings on the throne. Despite the conditional elements, the covenant with David was ultimately unconditional. God guaranteed a Davidic king on the throne, and this promise was reaffirmed by the prophets. Still, the covenant promise would be fulfilled only by an obedient king, and the New Testament claims that this person is Jesus of Nazareth. We see in the New Testament documents that Jesus is consistently proclaimed to be the Messiah and Lord as the crucified and risen one. As David's Son he is now reigning at God's right hand and will come again to consummate his reign. When he returns, all of God's covenant promises will be fulfilled.

6

The New Covenant

When we think of the new covenant, it needs to be understood in light of the storyline of Scripture as a whole. Thus, what is meant by the new covenant must not be limited merely to the phrase "new covenant." It is expressed in a variety of ways in the Prophets. The different terminology helps us comprehend that the new covenant embraces a number of different themes. We see the phrases "new covenant" (Jer. 31:31), "covenant of peace" (Isa. 54:10; Ezek. 34:25; 37:26), and "everlasting covenant" (Isa. 55:3; 61:8; Jer. 32:40; 50:5; Ezek. 16:60; 37:26). The significance of these phrases and other uses of *covenant* can be discerned only in context, and the explanation below will attempt to fill out some of the contextual elements present. In addition, some New Testament references to the new covenant, even where the exact term isn't used, will also be explored (Mark 14:24; Luke 22:20; 1 Cor. 11:25; 2 Cor. 3:6; Heb. 7:22; 8:6–13; 9:15; 10:16–18, 29; 12:24; 13:20).

The new covenant represents the fulfillment of God's covenants with his people. I should immediately add that the new covenant isn't actually the fulfillment of the covenant with Noah, for the covenant with Noah isn't redemptive per se but guarantees that history will endure so that the Lord can fulfill the saving promises found in the other covenants. The other covenants are not entirely carried over in the new covenant. The difference between them will be detailed below, but here it should be noted that the genealogical principle in the covenant with Abraham, signified by circumcision, is not continued in the new covenant. Hence, there is both continuity and discontinuity with the Abrahamic covenant.

Additionally, the new covenant is not simply a renewal of the covenant with Israel. I will argue that the new covenant is genuinely new, and thus the discontinuity between the new covenant and the covenant with Israel is greater than the continuity. The covenant with David also finds its realization in the new covenant, which is inaugurated in Jesus's blood, is fulfilled in the reign of Jesus from heaven in the present evil age, and is consummated in his reign over the entire cosmos in the age to come.

The new covenant also fulfills the mandates given to Adam and Eve in the covenant at creation. The entire universe is ruled by God through the God-man Jesus Christ. As a priest-king he has secured forgiveness of sins so that all those who belong to him will reign with him forever. Several themes must be considered to understand the new covenant: (1) renewal of heart; (2) regeneration; (3) complete forgiveness of sin; (4) new exodus, forgiveness of sins, and a new David; and (5) reunification of the people of God. Finally, we will examine how the new covenant fulfills all the previous covenants, except, as noted above, the covenant with Noah.

Renewal of Heart

We begin with Jeremiah 31:31–34, for it is the banner passage on the new covenant. Jeremiah contrasts the new covenant with the old, declaring that they should be distinguished. The old covenant is the one made with Israel, for the Lord reminds his people how he freed them from Egypt (v. 32). The flaw with the old covenant is that Israel failed to keep its stipulations (v. 32), so the covenant curses came on Israel and culminated in exile. The new covenant remedies this problem, however, for God promises to "put my law within them" and to "write it on their hearts" (v. 33). That is how the purpose of the covenant, which is fellowship with God, will be achieved: "I will be their God, and they shall be my people" (v. 33). The new covenant, then, makes provisions so that the people of God have a desire from within to keep God's commands.

Israel's new heart is tied up with return from exile, as we see clearly in Jeremiah 32:

> I will give them one heart and one way, that they may fear
> me forever, for their own good and the good of their children
> after them. I will make with them an everlasting covenant,
> that I will not turn away from doing good to them. And I will
> put the fear of me in their hearts, that they may not turn from
> me. I will rejoice in doing them good, and I will plant them
> in this land in faithfulness, with all my heart and all my soul.
> "For thus says the LORD: Just as I have brought all this great
> disaster upon this people, so I will bring upon them all the
> good that I promise them." (vv. 39–42)

When the new covenant arrives, Israel will be planted in the land and will not turn away from the Lord again. Incidentally, we see from this passage that Israel's return to the land in 1948 doesn't fulfill this prophecy, for Israel did not turn to the Lord or Jesus as the Messiah when they entered the land, and they have still not done so to this day.

The promise of a new heart and a new obedience is also found in Ezekiel 36:26–27: "I will give you a new heart, and a new spirit I will put within you. And I will remove the heart of stone from your flesh and give you a heart of flesh. And I will put my Spirit within you, and cause you to walk in my statutes and be careful to obey my rules." Under the old covenant Israel was bedeviled by "a heart of stone." In the new covenant God plants his Spirit within his people, and as a result they receive "a heart of flesh," "a new heart," and "a new spirit" (see also Ezek. 11:18–19). The gift of the Spirit enables the people of God to keep God's laws. The failure to obey that began with Adam in the garden is remedied by the new covenant.

New Testament writers pick up on this theme as well. Hebrews quotes the new-covenant prophecy of Jeremiah twice (8:8–12; 10:16–18). Paul contrasts the new covenant with the old in 2 Corinthians 3, and he clearly alludes to both Jeremiah 31 and Ezekiel 36 (2 Cor. 3:3, 6). The old covenant was written "on tablets of stone" (2 Cor. 3:3), which represents the Ten Commandments Moses received from the Lord. No criticism is lodged about the content of the commandments; they represent God's will (see Rom. 7:12). Still, the words of the commands are merely a "letter" (2 Cor. 3:6). Simply being taught the commands doesn't give anyone the ability to keep them. In the new covenant, however, believers are granted "the Spirit of the living God" (v. 3). Now the Spirit of life (v. 6) has been given to them, hence believers are transformed so that they are enabled to do God's will (cf. Rom. 7:1–8:4). Paul also makes this point in 1 Thessalonians 4:9 when he says believers are "taught by God to love one another." Paul almost certainly thinks of the new-covenant promise of Jeremiah here, for the love of God is inscribed on the heart. We can sum up the first dimension of the new covenant by saying that the hearts of the people of God are renewed by the Spirit of God.

A Regenerate Covenant People

The second feature of the new covenant is quite striking and is another way of describing the renewal of heart. In contrast to the old covenant, every member of the new covenant is regenerate. observation follows from the discussion above. What differentiates the old covenant from the new is that in the latter the members of the covenant are regenerated by God's Spirit. Jeremiah and Ezekiel describe this in different ways, but they point to the same reality. Jeremiah particularly stresses this point: "No longer shall each one teach his neighbor and each his brother, saying, 'Know the LORD,' for they shall all know me, from the least of them to the greatest"(Jer. 31:34). Striking here is the comprehensiveness of what Jeremiah says. Certainly people need teaching even after becoming believers. Jeremiah's point, however, is that they don't need to be instructed or commanded to know the Lord as if they are unconverted, for by definition all those in the new covenant know the Lord. Notice that Jeremiah says that this is true from the least to the greatest. In other words, there are no exceptions. Everyone in the new-covenant community is regenerate.

By way of contrast, members of the old covenant weren't necessarily regenerate. Certainly, the remnant was regenerated by the Lord (which is described in terms of the circumcision of the heart), but many were part of the covenant without being transformed. Children entered the covenant under the old administration without being regenerated. Here we see one of the most profound differences between the covenants. The covenant with Israel and the covenant with Abraham had a genealogical principle. All those born in Israel were covenant members if they were circumcised. Many in Israel (probably the majority, in fact, and thus the exile!) were part of the covenant without being regenerated. On the other hand, there is no such thing as a nonregenerated new-covenant member. First John 2 picks up on Jeremiah's promise that all new-covenant members have new life. John writes to assure his readers that they truly belong to God, that they genuinely have eternal life (1 John 5:13). He assures them, "You have been anointed by the Holy One, and you all have knowledge" (1 John 2:20). The anointing here refers to the work of God's Spirit in giving them life so that they have genuine knowledge of God. John refers to the same truth when he says a few verses later, "But the anointing that you received from him abides in you, and you have no need that anyone should teach you" (v. 27). John isn't saying that believers don't need any teachers whatsoever. He draws on Jeremiah's prophecy and makes the same point. Believers don't need anyone to teach them about receiving new life, for they have already been anointed by the Spirit and are converted members of the new-covenant community.

Jesus in the Gospel of John also teaches that members of the new-covenant community have new life. He says, "They will all be taught by God" (6:45). Jesus refers here to those who are effectively called, to those who were given by the Father to the Son, so that they come to Jesus and believe in him (John 6:35, 37, 44, 64–65). The prophecy of Isaiah is quoted here: "All your children shall be taught by the Lord" (Isa. 54:13). This prophecy is inserted in a context in which the Lord promises that Israel's offspring will flourish, which fulfills the promise of offspring made to Abraham. Notice again the universality of the new-covenant promise. "All the children" will receive the saving teaching, all the children will be anointed with the Spirit, and Jesus applies this to those who are effectively called.

In the Old Testament we see that the Spirit is poured out on prophets, kings, and other leaders. There is a recognition, however, that the Spirit isn't distributed to all. Moses voices the hope that in the future the Spirit will be poured out more generally, responding to Joshua's concerns about some who had prophesied outside of the tent in the camp: "Would that all the Lord's people were prophets, that the Lord would put his Spirit on them" (Num. 11:29). Joel's prophecy represents the fulfillment of Moses's desire:

And it shall come to pass afterward, that I will pour out my
Spirit on all flesh; your sons and your daughters shall proph-
esy, your old men shall dream dreams, and your young men
shall see visions. Even on the male and female servants in
those days I will pour out my Spirit. (Joel 2:28–29)

Peter proclaims that Joel's prophecy was fulfilled on the day of
Pentecost (Acts 2:16–17). Distinctive about Joel's prophecy is that
the Spirit is poured out upon all: young and old, male and female.
The comprehensiveness and the universality of the Spirit's work in
the new covenant represents a striking contrast to the old covenant.

It is sometimes said that there is an *already but not yet* in the fulfillment of the new-covenant promise, which means that members of the
new covenant can still apostatize during this present evil age. Such a
reading places the *not yet* at the wrong place, for all who are foreknown,
predestined, called, and justified will be glorified (Rom. 8:29–30).
Another way of putting it is that the Spirit, which is the gift of the
new covenant to all covenant members, is the guarantee of the final
inheritance (2 Cor. 1:22; Eph. 1:13–14; 4:30). Therefore, the *not yet*
of the new covenant isn't that some members can and do apostatize,
for God protects by his power all those who belong to him (1 Pet.
1:5; cf. Phil. 1:6). The *not yet* is that though the Spirit regenerates and
indwells every new-covenant member, they are not yet completely
transformed. Their obedience, though genuine and supernatural, is
not yet perfect. Complete sanctification and holiness will be theirs on
the final day, on the day of redemption (see 1 Thess. 5:23–24). Even
now, however, all new-covenant members are regenerate.

Complete Forgiveness of Sin

Another feature of the new covenant is final and complete forgiveness of sins. Jeremiah emphasizes this element of the new covenant:

"I will forgive their iniquity, and I will remember their sin no more" (Jer. 31:34). Under the old covenant, sacrifices were offered for the forgiveness of sin (Leviticus 1–7), and on the Day of Atonement sacrifices were offered to cleanse the priests and people of sins committed in the year that had just passed (Leviticus 16). The author of Hebrews especially picks up on this theme in chapters 8–10 and quotes the new-covenant promise from Jeremiah twice (Heb. 8:8–12; 10:16–18). A frequent word in Hebrews is *better*, and this fits with the superiority of the new covenant over the old. In Jesus there are "a better hope" (7:19), "a better covenant" (7:22; 8:6), "better promises" (8:6), "better sacrifices" (9:23), "a better possession" (10:34), "a better country" (11:16), "a better resurrection" (11:35 HCSB), and "a better word" (12:24). All of these better things are obtained by virtue of Jesus's sacrifice, which demonstrates that he is a better priest than any priest in the old covenant.

Jesus's sacrifice is superior because he entered God's very presence ("the greater and more perfect tent," Heb. 7:25); i.e., he "entered the most holy place once for all" with his own blood (Heb. 9:12 HCSB). Old-covenant sacrifices were offered in an earthly tent, but Jesus secured "eternal redemption" with his sacrifice (9:12). The Old Testament priesthood was weak and inadequate because it didn't bring us into God's presence (7:11–12, 18–19). Jesus, on the other hand, "is able to save to the uttermost those who draw near to God through him" (7:25). His sacrifice saves completely because he is a perfect priest, and his one sacrifice atones for sins forever (7:26–27). To put it another way, Jesus wins "eternal redemption" for his people (9:12) because he "offered himself" "through the eternal Spirit" (9:14). Jesus mediates a new covenant through his atoning death (9:15–22). His sacrifice brings us into God's presence in contrast to Old Testament sacrifices, which functioned as types and anticipations of Christ's sacrifice (9:23–24). Christ's one sacrifice atoned for sins decisively once for all (9:28; 10:10). Christ sits at God's right hand because final and complete sacrifice has been offered to atone for sins (10:12). We read in 10:14, "By a single offering he has perfected for all time those who are being sanctified." Since forgiveness has been secured once for all by Christ's death, no further offering is needed (10:18).

One of the most dramatic differences between the old covenant and the new covenant is evident here. Old-covenant sacrifices were offered repeatedly, for they didn't truly effect forgiveness. Christ's sacrifice was offered once, for by his death he dealt with sin completely and definitively. To put this another way, under the old covenant free and total access to God wasn't granted. God's presence was specially in the Most Holy Place in the tabernacle/temple, and it was accessed by the high priest only once a year (Leviticus 16; Heb. 9:6–8). By way of contrast, Jesus's once-for-all sacrifice truly cleanses the conscience of his people (Heb. 9:9, 14; 10:22), and thus we can approach God's throne boldly and with confidence (4:16; 10:19). Hence, believers are exhorted, "Let us draw near with a true heart in full assurance of faith, with our hearts sprinkled clean from an evil conscience and our bodies washed with pure water" (10:22). The new covenant is clearly superior to the old covenant since it grants free and confident access to God by virtue of Jesus's death.

In the new covenant we enjoy a better mediator, one who accomplishes full forgiveness of sins. We see this as well in the inauguration of the eucharist at the Last Supper. Jesus took the cup and said, "This cup that is poured out for you is the new covenant in my blood" (Luke 22:20). The cup hearkens back to the Old Testament where the cup regularly stands for the wrath of God, which is poured out on those who have rebelled and sinned against him (Ps. 11:6; 75:8; Isa. 51:17, 22; Jer. 25:15, 17, 28; 49:12; Lam. 4:21; Ezek. 23:31–33; Hab. 2:16). The reference to blood shows that Jesus's death is conceived of as a sacrifice. He spills his blood as a sacrificial victim, taking upon himself the wrath deserved by human beings. Since Jesus pronounced these words at a Passover meal, we see that Jesus saw his death as a Passover sacrifice (1 Cor. 5:7). Indeed, Jesus is the last and best Passover sacrifice, the means by which destruction is averted for those who belong to him, and thus all those who belong to Jesus are assured that they stand in the right before the Holy One of Israel.

New Exodus, Forgiveness of Sins, and a New David

Another complementary way of thinking of the new covenant is to see the link between the promise of a new exodus in the new covenant, the coming of a new David, and the forgiveness of sins.

First, we need to see the promise of a new exodus in the new-covenant promises. The new-covenant promise is found in Jeremiah 31:31–34, as we have seen, but that promise must be linked with the whole of what is sometimes called Jeremiah's "book of comfort." In Jeremiah the new covenant is inextricably tied to return from exile, as we can see from the following texts.

> For behold, days are coming, declares the LORD, when I will restore the fortunes of my people, Israel and Judah, says the LORD, and I will bring them back to the land that I gave to their fathers, and they shall take possession of it. (Jer. 30:3)

> Behold, I will save you from far away,
>   and your offspring from the land of their captivity.
> Jacob shall return and have quiet and ease,
>   and none shall make him afraid. (Jer. 30:10)

> Behold, I will restore the fortunes of the tents of Jacob
>   and have compassion on his dwellings;
> the city shall be rebuilt on its mound,
>   and the palace shall stand where it used to be. (Jer. 30:18)

Many other texts could be cited from Jeremiah to show that Israel would return from exile (e.g., 31:4–9, 17, 21, 23–24, 38–40; 32:15, 37–44; 33:7–13). At the same time, it is clear that Israel went into exile because of their sin, and they needed God's forgiveness to be restored. The Lord says:

> I have dealt you the blow of an enemy,
>> the punishment of a merciless foe,
> because your guilt is great,
>> because your sins are flagrant.
> Why do you cry out over your hurt?
>> Your pain is incurable.
> Because your guilt is great,
>> because your sins are flagrant,
>> I have done these things to you. (Jer. 30:14–15)

Israel's fundamental problem wasn't political but spiritual; they departed from the Lord's ways, and thus they experienced exile. "But they did not obey your voice or walk in your law. They did nothing of all you commanded them to do. Therefore you have made all this disaster come upon them" (Jer. 32:23). We find this stinging indictment as well:

> For the children of Israel and the children of Judah have done nothing but evil in my sight from their youth. The children of Israel have done nothing but provoke me to anger by the work of their hands, declares the LORD. This city has aroused my anger and wrath, from the day it was built to this day, so that I will remove it from my sight because of all the evil of the children of Israel and the children of Judah that they did to provoke me to anger—their kings and their officials, their priests and their prophets, the men of Judah and the inhabitants of

Jerusalem. They have turned to me their back and not their face. And though I have taught them persistently, they have not listened to receive instruction. (Jer. 32:30–33)

Israel's restoration can be ascribed only to the Lord's healing grace (30:17–18). He must redeem his people from their guilt and sin. "For the LORD has ransomed Jacob / and has redeemed him from hands too strong for him" (Jer. 31:11). Restoration will not come without forgiveness. "I will cleanse them from all the guilt of their sin against me, and I will forgive all the guilt of their sin and rebellion against me" (Jer. 33:8).

At the same time, the new covenant is linked with the coming of a new David. When the day of liberation comes, Israel will "serve the LORD their God and David their king" (Jer. 30:9). The return from exile is accompanied by a new leader: "I will cause a righteous Branch to spring up for David" (Jer. 33:15). Israel's salvation and righteousness will come not from themselves, for the Lord will be their righteousness (33:16), and the covenant with David will be fulfilled forever (33:17–20). We are reminded of the prophecy in Jeremiah 23:5–6:

Behold, the days are coming, declares the LORD, when I will raise up for David a righteous Branch, and he shall reign as king and deal wisely, and shall execute justice and righteousness in the land. In his days Judah will be saved, and Israel will dwell securely. And this is the name by which he will be called: "The LORD is our righteousness."

We see three new-covenant themes in Jeremiah. First, Israel was plunged into exile because of sin. Second, God would forgive Israel and restore them from exile. Third, God would raise up for them a new David. When we consider the New Testament witness, it is clear that the forgiveness contemplated in Jeremiah is accomplished by Jesus Christ. We have seen this theme very clearly in Hebrews 8–10. Jesus is the new David, and forgiveness of sins comes only through him. The new covenant, in other words, is established on the basis of Jesus's atoning sacrifice.

Ezekiel also prophesies the return of Israel to its land:

> But you, O mountains of Israel, shall shoot forth your branches and yield your fruit to my people Israel, for they will soon come home. For behold, I am for you, and I will turn to you, and you shall be tilled and sown. And I will multiply people on you, the whole house of Israel, all of it. The cities shall be inhabited and the waste places rebuilt. (Ezek. 36:8–10; cf. 36:35–36; 37:12, 21, 25)

Ezekiel, like Jeremiah, maintains that Israel went into exile because of sin:

> Son of man, when the house of Israel lived in their own land, they defiled it by their ways and their deeds. Their ways before me were like the uncleanness of a woman in her menstrual impurity. So I poured out my wrath upon them for the blood that they had shed in the land, for the idols with which they had defiled it. I scattered them among the nations, and they were dispersed through the countries. In accordance with their ways and their deeds I judged them. (Ezek. 36:17–19)

The famous text, Ezekiel 36:24–28, which promises the Spirit to enable God's people to obey his instructions, also promises return from exile. The Lord assures Israel that he will cleanse them from guilt (36:29, 33; 37:23). When God restores his people, "one king shall be king over them" (37:22), and "my servant David shall be king over them, and they shall all have one shepherd. They shall walk in my rules and be careful to obey my statutes" (Ezek. 37:24). Restoration from exile, forgiveness, and the new David will become a reality when God makes "a covenant of peace" and "an everlasting covenant" (37:26). Then God will dwell with his people, and the covenant purpose will be realized: "I will be their God, and they shall be my people" (37:27).

Isaiah doesn't use the expression "new covenant," but the expressions "covenant of peace" (54:10) and "everlasting covenant" (55:3; 61:8) are two ways of expressing the same notion (see also 42:6; 49:8; 59:21). Both of these expressions are found in Isaiah 40–66, which features the theme of a new exodus from Babylon. We read in Isaiah 51:11, "The ransomed of the LORD shall return / and come to Zion with singing; / everlasting joy shall be upon their heads; / they shall obtain gladness and joy, / and sorrow and sighing shall flee away" (see also 40:3–11; 42:16; 43:2, 5–7, 16–21; 48:20–21; 49:6–11).

Isaiah also emphasizes that Israel went into exile because of sin:

> Who gave up Jacob to the looter,
>   and Israel to the plunderers?
> Was it not the LORD, against whom we have sinned,
>   in whose ways they would not walk,
>   and whose law they would not obey?
> So he poured on him the heat of his anger
>   and the might of battle;
> it set him on fire all around, but he did not understand;
>   it burned him up, but he did not take it to heart.
>   (Isa. 42:24–25)

We see the same theme when the Lord says to Israel, "You have burdened me with your sins; / you have wearied me with your iniquities" (Isa. 43:24). Sin stained Israel's life from the beginning and explains why they were exiled: "Your first father sinned, / and your mediators transgressed against me. / Therefore I will profane the princes of the sanctuary, / and deliver Jacob to utter destruction / and Israel to reviling" (vv. 27–28). Israel's sin regularly crops up in Isaiah's prophecies (46:8; 48:1–2, 4; 50:1–2; 52:3–5; 57:3–13; 58:1; 59:1–15; 64:6; 65:2–7; 66:3–4).

Isaiah also refers to a coming Davidic king in the first part of his book (see 9:2–7; 11:1–10), but we don't see the Davidic theme as explicitly in the second part. But we do see that the Lord will restore his people by forgiving their sins (43:25; 44:22). What stands out in Isaiah is the role of the servant in taking upon himself the sin of Israel. First, the servant is identified as Israel (41:8–9; 42:19; 43:10; 44:1–2, 21; 45:4; 48:20). It becomes apparent, however, as the prophecy proceeds that the servant and Israel are not coterminous, for the servant will bring Israel and Jacob back to the Lord (49:3). In Isaiah 50 the servant suffers (v. 6), but unlike Israel, who suffered for their own guilt, the servant isn't guilty of transgression (v. 9), and therefore he expects to be vindicated by the Lord (vv. 7–9). The servant is an obedient disciple, eager and ready to do the Lord's will (vv. 4–5). Indeed, the servant bears the punishment Israel deserves and suffers in their place:

> Surely he has borne our griefs
>   and carried our sorrows;
> yet we esteemed him stricken,
>   smitten by God, and afflicted.
> But he was pierced for our transgressions;
>   he was crushed for our iniquities;
> upon him was the chastisement that brought us peace,
>   and with his wounds we are healed.
> All we like sheep have gone astray;
>   we have turned—every one—to his own way;

and the Lord has laid on him
    the iniquity of us all. (53:4–6)

At the end of the day, the servant will triumph (v. 10), and "many [will] be accounted righteous" since "he shall bear their iniquities" (v. 11; cf. v. 12). The promise of many "offspring" (v. 10) becomes a reality through the servant. It is not surprising that the next chapter of Isaiah speaks of the "covenant of peace" (54:10), for Israel's forgiveness, restoration, and the promise of a new Jerusalem (60:1–22; 62:1–12) and a new creation (65:17; 66:22) are secured through the death and resurrection of the servant.

As the New Testament reflects on these three themes, we see that the restoration of God's people and the forgiveness of sins occur through the death and resurrection of Jesus. He is the servant of the Lord who atones for the transgressions of his people. We see an allusion to the servant theme in Mark 10:45: "For even the Son of Man came not to be served but to serve, and to give his life as a ransom for many." Jesus suffered in the place of many to free them from bondage to sin. The word *redemption* in the New Testament hearkens back to the exodus in Egypt and thus the New Testament witness points forward to the new exodus Jesus won for this people. Paul declares in Colossians 1:13–14 that God "has delivered us from the domain of darkness and transferred us to the kingdom of his beloved Son, in whom we have redemption, the forgiveness of sins." The new exodus has been accomplished through the forgiveness of sins, and that redemption has been accomplished in the death of Jesus Christ by which he propitiated the wrath of God with his blood (Rom. 3:24–26; see also Eph. 1:7).

We could point to a number of passages in the New Testament where Jesus is identified as the servant of the Lord, but Peter's words in his first letter are particularly clear:

He committed no sin, neither was deceit found in his mouth. When he was reviled, he did not revile in return; when he suffered, he did not threaten, but continued entrusting himself to him who judges justly. He himself bore our sins in his body on the tree, that we might die to sin and live to righteousness. By his wounds you have been healed. For you were straying like sheep, but have now returned to the Shepherd and Overseer of your souls. (1 Pet. 2:22–25)

The allusions to Isaiah 53 are multiple and obvious, showing that atonement and forgiveness are based on Jesus's death in our place.

The new covenant has been fulfilled in Jesus Christ, since he fulfills the prophecies made about the coming of David. The Davidic covenant, as we saw in chapter 5, points to Jesus Christ. As the Christ, Jesus took upon himself the sin of the people of God, and thus he accomplished the new and true exodus, which means that redemption and freedom from sin are now a reality. Exile and separation from God, as we see from Adam onward, is due to sin. Return from exile, restoration to fellowship with God, comes only where there is forgiveness, and Jesus brings such forgiveness by his sacrifice.

Reunification of the People of God

Another blessing of the new covenant is the reunification of the people of God. Israel was divided into two kingdoms (Judah and Israel) around 930 BC after Solomon's reign. The division occurred because of Solomon's sin and idolatry. The northern kingdom of Israel suffered exile at the hands of the Assyrians in 722 BC, and the southern kingdom of Judah went into exile at the impetus of the Babylonians in 586 BC. Ezekiel looks forward to a day when the Spirit will revive the dry bones of Israel, and Ezekiel ties this to Israel's restoration to the land (37:1–14). Ezekiel then turns to the division between

Israel and Judah (vv. 15–28). The kingdoms of Israel and Judah are represented by two sticks (v. 16). What Yahweh will do, however, is make the two sticks into one stick (vv. 17–19), which means that Israel and Judah will be restored to the land and be one nation with one king (vv. 20–22). The division between the two nations, which had continued for hundreds of years, will come to an end. The restoration will take place on the basis of the forgiveness and cleansing of their sins (v. 23). Then the covenant relationship always intended will be a reality: "They shall be my people, and I will be their God" (v. 23). David will rule over the united kingdom, and the nation will keep God's rules (v. 24). Clearly, the reference to David refers to a new David who is coming, and this new David "shall be their prince forever" (v. 25). God will dwell in the midst of his people and his "sanctuary" will be in their midst forever (vv. 27–28).

New Testament writers see this prophecy fulfilled in Jesus. Clearly, he is the new David noted by Ezekiel. The reconciliation of the northern and southern kingdoms is found in Acts 8. The Samaritans were separated from Israel and lived in Samaria. They had built their own temple on Mount Gerizim (John 4:20–21), though it was burned down by John Hyrcanus about 110 BC. The Samaritans didn't fellowship with Jews who worshiped in the Jerusalem temple (John 4:9). Samaritans refused to receive Jesus as he traveled to Jerusalem, and James and John wanted Jesus to call fire from heaven to consume them, but Jesus reproved them for their vengeful attitude (Luke 9:52–56). When Jews desired to insult Jesus, they hurled the epithet "Samaritan" at him (John 8:48). Philip, one of the seven (Acts 6:1–6), proclaimed the gospel in Samaria after the death of Stephen (Acts 8:4–25).

The mission was extraordinarily successful, and many believed that Jesus was the Christ. Even though the Samaritans put their faith in Jesus, they didn't receive the Spirit when they believed. Such a separation between belief in Jesus and the reception of the Spirit is witnessed nowhere else in the New Testament, and thus this unique event cries out for an explanation. What is remarkable is that Philip, one of the seven, couldn't bestow the Spirit. Instead, the Spirit was granted to the Samaritans only when the apostles Peter and John laid their hands on them. Why was the Spirit withheld until Peter and John came down to Samaria? The best answer is that the Lord wanted to preserve the unity of the early church. He didn't want Samaritan and Jerusalem branches to develop in the church, so he made clear from the outset that the Samaritan church was under apostolic authority. The Spirit was bequeathed only through the apostles. What we see, then, is the fulfillment of Ezekiel's prophecy. The two sticks of the north and the south, Samaria and Judea, are now united in Jesus Christ. The unity of north and south is signaled by the summary statement found in Acts 9:31: "So the church throughout all Judea and Galilee and Samaria had peace and was being built up. And walking in the fear of the Lord and in the comfort of the Holy Spirit, it multiplied."

The next question is how this restoration relates to the influx of the Gentiles into the church. The Old Testament prophecies about the new covenant and the covenant of peace declare that Israel and Judah will be restored, that Israel will return to the land, and that Israel will be united. How is it that New Testament writers see the new covenant fulfilled in the church of Jesus Christ if the promise was originally made to Israel, especially since so many believers in these early days were Gentiles? It is quite clear that New Testament writers see the new covenant as inaugurated with the death and resurrection of Jesus Christ and the gift of the Spirit (Luke 22:30; 1 Cor. 11:25; 2 Cor. 3:6; Heb. 8:8–12; 10:16–18; 12:24), but how can promises made to Israel be fulfilled in the church of Jesus Christ, which is made up of both Jews and Gentiles? The answer of the New

Testament is that the church of Jesus Christ is restored Israel. A number of lines of argument make this case.

In Galatians 3:6–9 and Romans 4:9–22 we see that those who believe in Jesus Christ are the children of Abraham. Gentile believers are not merely outsiders participating in the promise. They are counted as the children of Abraham; they are part of restored Israel. They aren't merely beneficiaries of the promise made to Abraham; they *are* the children of Abraham. In the same way, in Galatians 6:16 believers in Jesus Christ are identified as the Israel of God. The verse is disputed, but identifying the church as the Israel of God fits far better with the message of Galatians as a whole. The false teachers insisted that Gentiles get circumcised and become Jews to enter God's people. Paul teaches that circumcision and becoming a Jewish convert are not necessary; they are children of Abraham by faith (Gal. 3:6–9), and they are members of the Israel of God if they are part of the new creation (Gal. 6:15). The restored Israel consists of both Jews and Gentiles who believe in Jesus Christ.

We see something quite similar in Romans 2:25–29, where the issue of circumcision surfaces. We learn from Paul that true circumcision is a matter of the heart and a work of the Holy Spirit. Paul says the same thing about being a true Jew:

> For no one is a Jew who is merely one outwardly, nor is circumcision outward and physical. But a Jew is one inwardly, and circumcision is a matter of the heart, by the Spirit, not by the letter. His praise is not from man but from God. (Rom. 2:28–29)

If true Jewishness and true circumcision are matters of the heart and the work of the Holy Spirit, then Gentile believers who have been transformed by the Holy Spirit are true Jews and truly circumcised! (Rom. 2:26). If they are truly circumcised and truly Jews, then they are covenant members; they are part of restored Israel. Physical circumcision, which was required in the covenant with Abraham and Israel, is no longer required with the onset of the new covenant. What matters is circumcision of the heart, the circumcision effected by the Spirit of God (Phil. 3:3). Another indication that the new covenant differs from the old is that every member of the new covenant community has a circumcised heart because of the work of the Holy Spirit. And Gentiles who are spiritually circumcised are true Jews.

The notion that the church of Jesus Christ, made up of both Jews and Gentiles, is restored Israel is also taught in Ephesians 2:11–3:13. Here Paul reflects on his apostolic ministry, particularly the mystery that he has been appointed to understand and explain to others (Eph. 3:6). The Gentiles during the old covenant administration were "alienated from the commonwealth of Israel and strangers to the covenants of promise" (2:12). They didn't have the promise of the Christ, had no hope, and were without God (2:12). But through the death of Jesus Christ, Gentiles have been brought near to God (2:13). The "hostility" between Jews and Gentiles has ended, and they are now "one" (2:14). The law with its commandments has been abolished (2:15), which means that the covenant made with Israel at Sinai is no longer in force. In the old covenant ethnic Israel constituted the people of God, but now there is "one new man" in Christ Jesus (2:15). In other words, Jesus is the true Israel, and the restored Israel is marked out by those who belong to him.

We see the same thought in Galatians 3:16. Jesus is the true offspring of Abraham, and thus all those who are Abraham's offspring (vv. 14, 29) belong to Jesus Christ by faith. Or, as Ephesians says, the hostility between Jews and Gentiles is terminated through the reconciling work of Jesus Christ (2:16). The unity of the people of God is established in Christ. Paul says to Gentiles, "You are no longer strangers and aliens, but you are fellow citizens with the saints and members of the household of God" (2:19). Notice that Gentiles are members of God's household, which means that they are equally members with the Jews. There are not two peoples of God but one people composed of both Jews and Gentiles. Together they constitute "a holy temple in the Lord" (2:21). Paul puts the same truth another way, where he discloses the mystery to his readers: "This mystery is that the Gentiles are fellow heirs, members of the same body, and partakers of the promise in Christ Jesus through the gospel" (Eph. 3:6).

In "the covenants of promise" (Eph. 2:12), which include the covenants with Abraham, Israel, and David, it wasn't clear what the status of Gentiles would be when the promises were fulfilled. The mystery, which was previously hidden but has now been eschatologically revealed, is that Gentiles are equally and fully members of the same body and fellow heirs with the Jews. We don't have two different bodies joined together but the same body united through Jesus Christ and in the gospel. Gentiles don't subscribe to the law to enter the people of God but are inducted into the people of God through Jesus himself. Jesus Christ as the new and true Israel unites the true Israel, which becomes a reality in him.

The same truth is communicated in the picture of the olive tree in Romans 11:17–24. The olive tree depicts the people of God, and both Jewish and Gentile branches are on the same tree. We don't have two different trees that have somehow merged. Rather, we have branches from different ethnic backgrounds, both Jew and Gentile, which now form one tree in Jesus Christ.

We see something similar in the fulfillment of Hosea's prophecy (Hos. 1:9–2:1) about the restoration of Israel, in Romans 9:25–26: "Those who were not my people I will call 'my people,' and her who was not beloved I will call 'beloved.'" And in the very place where it was said to them, 'You are not my people,' there they will be called 'sons of the living God.'" In its historical context in Hosea, the prophecy is about God's grace being poured out on Israel. Even though they are being judged because of their sin, the promise of Abraham (that they will be as many as the sand of the sea) will be fulfilled. What is remarkable, however, is that Paul sees this promise as fulfilled in the calling of Gentiles. There is no evidence that fulfillment occurred in an analogous way. Instead, the fulfillment is the calling of the Gentiles to faith.

We see a similar use of these Hosea verses in 1 Peter. Peter writes to Gentile believers and says, "Once you were not a people, but now you are God's people; once you had not received mercy, but now you have received mercy" (2:10). The promise is not limited to Gentile believers, of course; Jews who believe in Christ are also part of the olive tree (Rom. 11:17–24). In any case, the use of Hosea in the New Testament functions as further evidence that Jewish and Gentile believers constitute restored Israel.

We have another hint that ethnic Israel doesn't consist of the people of God in Paul's phrase, "Israel according to flesh," which suggests that there is an Israel according to the Spirit that transcends ethnic Israel. Even more compelling is the curious use of the word "Gentiles"; for instance, Peter can say to Gentile readers, "Keep your conduct among the Gentiles honorable" (1 Pet. 2:12). Elsewhere he exhorts his readers to turn from the old way of life that characterized them before their conversion: "For the time that is past suffices for doing what the Gentiles want to do" (1 Pet. 4:3). "Gentiles" for Peter has become a term to designate unbelievers, and Gentile readers are conceived to be part of Israel. This is confirmed by 1 Peter 2:10, as noted above. It is further substantiated by 1 Peter 2:9: "But you are a chosen race, a royal priesthood, a holy nation, a people for his own possession." Peter applies the term given to Israel in Exodus 19:6 to his Gentile readers. The Gentiles are no longer Gentiles! They are

Israel, at least spiritually speaking. Clearly, the church of Jesus Christ is the restored Israel or the new Israel in the sense that it fulfills the new-covenant promises made about Israel. The promise of the multiplication of offspring made to Abraham is fulfilled in the church of Jesus Christ, which consists of both Jewish and Gentile believers.

The last example of Gentile believers being identified as restored Israel is found in Revelation 7:1–8, where John refers to 144,000 and lists twelve thousand from the twelve tribes of Israel. Many interpreters think John refers to ethnic Israel here, but there are decisive reasons to think otherwise.

First, numbers in apocalyptic literature are regularly symbolic. Here we have the number twelve, which represents the people of God from the twelve tribes in the Old Testament, and the number is squared and then multiplied by one thousand. Hence, the number should be understood as a symbolic way of designating the entire people of God. Second, John follows a pattern found in Revelation 5. He is *told* about a lion (5:5), but *sees* a lamb (5:6), and the lion and the lamb are the same entity. So too here, John *hears* the number 144,000 (7:4), but he *sees* an uncountable multitude (7:9). Again, we have two different ways of describing the same entity, and the uncountable multitude buttresses the point that the 144,000 represent all believers.

Third, specifying twelve thousand from the tribes of Israel doesn't signify that they are literally Jews. John has already said twice that the Jews are a synagogue of Satan (2:9; 3:9), and the roles between unbelieving Jews and Christians have been reversed, so that now unbelieving Jews play the role of Gentiles in the Old Testament—they will bow before Christians and acknowledge that they are the loved ones, the elect ones of the Lord (3:9; cf. Deut. 7:7–8; Isa. 41:8). Fourth, a practical problem arises if the reference is to twelve thousand from twelve literal tribes of Israel. Genealogies are no longer known from the twelve tribes. In any case, virtually no Jews today know from what tribe they descend. If someone were to say that God knows the tribes, and they end up being exactly twelve thousand from each tribe, it is difficult to see how that statement would be meaningful. No one on earth will recognize that the twelve thousand are from the twelve tribes specified, for no one knows from what tribe they descend.

Fifth, in Revelation 14:3 the 144,000 are described as those "redeemed from the earth" and in 14:4 as having been "redeemed from mankind as firstfruits for God and the Lamb." The redeemed are most naturally interpreted to refer to *all* the redeemed, which consists of both Jews and Gentiles. Sixth, John says they are "virgins" who have "not defiled themselves with women" (14:4). But surely this language is symbolic, for virginity is not more pleasing to God than marriage, and it is false teachers who say that sexual relations within marriage are *defiling* (1 Tim. 4:3). John reaches back to the Old Testament, which often warns Israel against spiritual prostitution. To be devoted to God is to be a "pure virgin" devoted "to Christ" (2 Cor. 11:2). For all these reasons, then, we have good grounds for thinking that the number 144,000 is laden with imagery and symbolism, referring to the entire people of God as the new Israel.

The New Covenant and the Covenant of Creation

Since the new covenant is the consummation and fulfillment of the previous covenants, it should prove helpful to unpack how it relates to the covenants we have studied. There is some overlap here, but for the sake of clarity a review of these matters should prove useful. The covenant of creation made Adam and Eve responsible to rule the world for God as priest-kings in the garden temple. The sin of Adam and Eve plunged the world into chaos, so that both they and creation were corrupted by sin (Genesis 3). The new covenant fulfills the covenant with creation, for now the last Adam, Jesus Christ, has obeyed where Adam failed (Rom. 5:12–19; 1 Cor. 15:21–22). He was the obedient one who always did his Father's will, and thus his life was without sin.

In Jesus, God's purpose for human beings is realized. Adam was God's priest-king in the garden, and now Jesus is God's priest-king in the new creation, the new universe, the new temple. Adam was God's son, but Jesus is God's obedient son. Hence, Jesus, as the God-man, is crowned as Lord over all creation. All those who are united to Jesus Christ by faith rule over the new creation with him, for he is the true Son of Man in whom the saints enjoy the rule first promised to Adam (Dan. 7:13–27). The command to be fruitful and multiply is fulfilled in the many sons and daughters that belong to Jesus (Heb. 2:10–18). We see here how profoundly the covenants are interrelated, for the promise of land, offspring, and blessing given to Abraham are also elements of the covenant at creation. The land for Adam was the garden-temple, but the garden points to and is fulfilled in the new creation. The offspring promised to Adam and Eve (Gen. 3:15) is Jesus Christ; he is the offspring of the woman who triumphs over the Devil by his death and resurrection, and those who are united to Jesus Christ by faith and obedience also enjoy the promise that God will be their God and they will be his people. The blessing is not restricted to the garden, nor is it restricted to Israel's return from exile in Canaan, but now it embraces the entire creation. The entire world is a garden-temple over which God reigns.

The New Covenant and the Covenant with Noah

How does the new covenant relate to the Noahic covenant? The primary purpose of the Noahic covenant was to preserve the world so that God's saving promises would be realized. We saw many continuities between the covenant at creation and the Noahic covenant, which suggests that the covenant with Noah was a resumption of sorts of the covenant at creation. The covenants are different as well, of course, since sin had intervened. Therefore, there are provisions introduced in the Noahic covenant, such as the role of government, which aren't included in the covenant with creation.

So how does the covenant with Noah relate to the new covenant? The call to be fruitful and multiply, which is reiterated in the Noahic covenant, along with the call to exercise dominion over the world, is fulfilled in the new covenant in Jesus Christ. Also, in Isaiah 54:9–10, Isaiah says the promise of future peace is as certain as the fulfillment of the promises made in the Noahic covenant. The mass of humanity that is saved enjoys salvation through Jesus Christ, who exercises a just and loving dominion over the new universe.

The New Covenant and the Covenant with Abraham

The fundamental elements of the covenant with Abraham are off-spring, land, and blessing. The promise of offspring is fulfilled in the new covenant in Jesus Christ. He is the true offspring of Abraham, for he is the obedient one. We saw in considering the covenant with Abraham that one reason Abraham was blessed was his obedience. Still, Abraham fell short of what God required, so the promises made to Abraham are realized in a climactic sense in Jesus Christ. It is also plain in the new covenant that those who are the true children of Abraham (Gal. 3:6–9; Rom. 4:9–12; Heb. 2:16) belong to the people of God through faith in Jesus Christ. Hence, the promise that Abraham's offspring would be as many as the stars of the sky and as numerous as the sand of the sea comes to fruition through the cross and resurrection of Jesus Christ and through the work of the Holy Spirit who is poured out as a result of Jesus's triumph over the Devil.

The land promised to Abraham was Canaan, but in the new creation the land promise is realized in Jesus Christ. His resurrection from the dead (Rom. 1:4; 1 Cor. 15:1–28) signals the arrival of the new creation in an already but not yet way. The new creation arrives in its fullness when those who trust in Jesus are raised from the dead because of their union with Christ. The land promise, the new creation, is then widened to the entire universe, which will become God's city and temple (Rev. 21:1–22:5).

God and the Lamb will reign over all creation, and the universal blessing promised to Abraham will be achieved. Everything in the universe will be reconciled to God (Col. 1:20). Rebellion will no longer be allowed in the universe. Universal reconciliation doesn't mean all will be saved. The book of Revelation and many other passages make clear that many will experience the second death, the lake of fire. Universal reconciliation means that all God's enemies will be pacified, domesticated, and put in their place. The entire world will enjoy the beneficent rule of the true son of Abraham, the Son of God and Son of Man—the rule of Jesus Christ the Lord.

The New Covenant and the Covenant with Israel

What is the relationship between the new covenant and the covenant with Israel? It is one of continuity and discontinuity; there is a fulfillment and a setting aside. Of course, the same can be said about all the covenants. When the covenant with Abraham is fulfilled, there is also discontinuity, for the genealogical principle of that covenant passes away. Circumcision is no longer required. Physical circumcision in the covenant with Israel is fulfilled in the circumcision of the heart. Similarly, the sacrifices required point forward typologically to the sacrifice of Christ.

The purity and food laws that separated Israel from the nations anticipate the holiness with which the people of God are to live (1 Cor. 5:6–8; 1 Pet. 1:15–16). The tabernacle and temple culminate in Jesus Christ as the true temple and in the people of God as God's temple (1 Cor. 3:16; Eph. 2:19–22; 1 Pet. 2:4–8). The New Testament clearly teaches that the old covenant is terminated with the arrival of the new covenant. Paul specifically identifies the covenant with Israel as "the old covenant" (2 Cor. 3:14). Hebrews says that the first covenant with Israel is "obsolete" (Heb. 8:13). The old covenant pointed toward and anticipated the new. In the old covenant Israel was separated from the nations, a distinct national and theocratic entity. But in the new covenant the people of God, the restored Israel, is made up of both Jews and Gentiles. In the old covenant Israel was God's son and firstborn (Ex. 4:22–23), but in the new covenant Jesus is the Son of God, and people become God's sons through faith in him.

In the old covenant the law was written on stony tablets, but in the new covenant the law is inscribed on the hearts of believers through the Holy Spirit. The obedience to God demanded in the old covenant is realized in the new covenant through the power of the Spirit, who is bestowed upon believers by virtue of Christ's atoning work, his resurrection, and his exaltation to God's right hand.

The New Covenant and the Covenant with David

The new covenant also fulfills the Davidic covenant. We saw earlier that the new-covenant promises are found in contexts where there is also the promise that a new David will come (cf. Jer. 23:5–6; 30:9; 33:15–22, 26; Ezek. 34:23–24; 37:24–25; cf. also Hos. 3:5; Amos 9:11). In the covenants there is a stream by which the promise is realized. Adam is son of God and priest-king. The promise of offspring who will triumph over the Serpent (Gen. 3:15) will be fulfilled in the Abrahamic covenant through the offspring of Abraham. Israel, as the descendant of Abraham, is God's son (Ex. 4:22–23) and functions as God's priest-king (Ex. 19:6). The promise is narrowed down further, so that the Davidic king is the true son of God (2 Sam. 7:14; Ps. 2:7, 12; Isa. 9:6). We saw indications even in the covenant with Abraham that kings would come from Abraham (cf. Gen. 17:6, 16;

35:11; 49:8–10; Num. 24:17). The promise of priesthood isn't left behind, for the Davidic heir will be both lord and priest in the order of Melchizedek (Ps. 110:1, 4). All these promises are again fulfilled in Jesus Christ. He is the true son of David, a priest-king, and the Lord of the world. All of God's promises made to Abraham are realized in him.

Conclusion

The new covenant represents the culmination of God's saving work among his people. God regenerates his people by his Spirit and renews their hearts so that they obey him. He is their God, and they are his people. The basis for such renewal is the cross and resurrection of Jesus Christ, for by his atoning death and resurrection complete forgiveness of sins is achieved. Hence, a new and bold access to God is obtained which wasn't available in the old covenant. The covenant with Israel passed away, and now the promise is fulfilled in the restored Israel, which consists of both Jews and Gentiles. Jesus is the last and second Adam who obeys where Adam failed, who brings his people into the new creation so that they can reign with him as priest-kings (cf. Dan. 7:18, 22, 27; 1 Cor. 6:2; 1 Pet. 2:9; Rev. 1:6; 5:10; 20:6).

The promises of Abraham are fulfilled in the new covenant that Jesus brings, for he is the true offspring of Abraham (Gal. 3:16), and all those who belong to him are the children of Abraham. The land promise is fulfilled in an inaugural way in his resurrection and then in a consummate way in the new creation. A new world of peace and righteousness is coming in which God and the Lamb will reign! God's purpose in creating human beings to rule the world for God will be fulfilled in Jesus Christ and all those who belong to him. In addition, the promise of universal blessing is fulfilled in the new creation, for salvation now reaches every tribe, tongue, people, and nation through Jesus's redeeming work (Rev. 5:9). The promise that David won't lack a man on the throne is fulfilled in Jesus Christ. He reigns now from heaven at God's right hand as the son of David, as Lord and Christ (Acts 2:32–36). And he will reign forever and ever over the new creation. "Amen. Come, Lord Jesus!" (Rev. 22:20).

For Further Reading

Dumbrell, William J. *Covenant and Creation: An Old Testament Covenantal Theology*. Rev. ed. Milton Keynes, England: Paternoster, 2013.

Gentry, Peter J., and Stephen J. Wellum. *Kingdom through Covenant: A Biblical-Theological Understanding of the Covenants*. Wheaton, IL: Crossway, 2012.

———. *God's Kingdom through God's Covenants: A Concise Biblical Theology*. Wheaton, IL: Crossway, 2015.

Horton, Michael. *God of Promise: Introducing Covenant Theology*. Grand Rapids, MI: Baker, 2006.

Robertson, O. Palmer. *The Christ of the Covenants*. Phillipsburg, NJ: Presbyterian & Reformed, 1980.

General Index

Scripture Index

Short Studies in Biblical Theology

This series is designed to help readers see the whole Bible as a unified story—culminating in Jesus.

Insightful, accessible, and practical, these books serve as bite-sized introductions to major subjects in biblical theology.

Visit crossway.org/SSBT for more information.